The Shelter

Finding Strength to Keep Watch

the Shelter

Finding Strength to Keep Watch

Billie Cash

AMBASSADOR INTERNATIONAL
GREENVILLE, SOUTH CAROLINA & BELFAST, NORTHERN IRELAND

www.ambassador-international.com

The Shelter

Finding Strength to Keep Watch

Printed in the United States of America
ISBN 978-1-935507-11-6

Cover Design & Page Layout by David Siglin of A&E Media

AMBASSADOR INTERNATIONAL
Emerald House
427 Wade Hampton Blvd.
Greenville, SC 29609, USA
www.ambassador-international.com

AMBASSADOR PUBLICATIONS
Providence House
Ardenlee Street
Belfast, BT6 8QJ, Northern Ireland, UK
www.ambassador-productions.com

The colophon is a trademark of Ambassador

DEDICATION

In honor of the men and women of our Armed Forces who have stood watch and paid the ultimate sacrifice in the name of freedom for America.

"The tree of liberty must be refreshed from time to time with the blood of patriots and tyrants."

— Thomas Jefferson

May the God of the SHELTER summon us to take our watch and follow Him.

"What God expects us to attempt, he also expects us to achieve."

— Dr. Stephen Olford

ENDORSEMENTS

"It is obvious that Billie drinks deeply from her cup of life and in the overflow she unselfishly refreshes others. In *The Shelter*, the constant awareness of the Savior's influence is on every page. Her love and devotion for her Lord creates in the reader a longing for greater intimacy with Him as she effortlessly transports us into the throne room of Heaven with her prayers. She gives expression to our deepest needs and concerns as women today. Thank you for obedience to our holy God in writing this book for such a time as this."

— MARIE KOLARCIK, LOUISVILLE, KY

Former Navy wife, mother of 6, Bible teacher, friend

Psalm 11:3 says, *When the foundations are being destroyed, what can the righteous do?* "Billie provides the answer in THE SHELTER. I trembled and wept for our nation as I read the book. We are not hopeless! God has not forsaken us…we have forsaken Him. I hear the warning. I sense the urgency. Count me in as one who will… arise, intercede and raise the banner for biblical living through the power of the Holy Spirit…for the sake of my children, their children, the people of this world…most importantly for the honor of His name. Billie, you beautifully and movingly built your case. You walked us through scripture to show us God's heart concerning His love and sovereignty over our lives. Heroes in the Bible like Paul and Esther surrendered their lives to the purposes of God and heroes in our nation like George Washington and Thomas Jefferson raised the standard of biblical truth. May we all stand guard and not allow religion to choke out the gospel in our lives. They stood their watch and so must we."

— HOPE ROBERTS, BAHAMA, NC.

"Thank you for writing the *SHELTER*. I did not want it to end. What an excellent book for America and for me. It has challenged me to step up and set goals. God will take me through. I have heard the trumpet. I have joined. I will not fret or lie down. Our God does reign. 'Living in His presence is living.'"

— STEPHANIE CARBAUGH, LANCASTER, PA.

"I have been blessed and spiritually uplifted beyond words with this book. Each time I came across the word *SHELTER*, I felt confidence, security, peace and the stability of the Lord's Presence. We will need both reason and faith to establish godliness for the generations that follow us. God will steer us through difficult times. Faith is our greatest comfort and our mightiest weapon. The days of weakness will come but in Jesus' Name we shall overcome together. The remainder of my life will be given to helping bring liberty to the home, the market place, the school, the family and the government. I cannot be silent!

As Billie reminded us, "Come to the *SHELTER*. Find His strength. Keep watch."

— NORMA SEIFERT, COLLIERVILLE, TN

Kansas State University – BA

Her credentials include organist, piano teacher 1951-1995, past president of Tennessee Music Teachers Association, Iowa Music Teachers Association and Western Central Division Music teachers National Association. She serves as a National board member for CWFA. Norma is mother to three adult children, grandmother to eight and great grand to three. Married to Robert P. Seifert, retired Senior VP Worldwide Research, Pioneer hybrid, Des Moines, IA.

"To live in today's uncertainty we must find the shelter of God's Presence day and night…. When we live there our faith will be fortified and we will be strengthened to keep watch." What insight you have given! You have spoken right to our hearts and challenged us through God's Word…giving us examples of Nehemiah, Paul as well as personal experience. I must keep watch over my faith in Christ, my family, and every aspect of my life… without ceasing. I am so blessed by this book! Thank you."

— DEANNA HOFFMANN, WAKE FOREST, NC

Wife and mother to four precious little ones, she and her husband are church planters who have served internationally for nine years. Presently they are beginning a new ministry in Northern part of America.

"Time is a gift and God uses nature, sound, and beauty as well as terror to awaken us to our need for truth and peace available in Christ. Waking up and keeping watch are the priorities of our day.

The way Billie proceeded to develop each thought is truly a gift from the Lord. He will touch many hearts through this book. The precious family stories bring us into your heart and God's... moving us forward from strength to strength...reconnecting us to the hope we have in Christ, I believe this book will kindle and rekindle the fire of passion for God. I thoroughly enjoyed the SHELTER."

— BETSY BILBRUCK COVINGTON, LA

A native of Illinois, this savvy world traveler and business woman is experienced in administration, human resources, public relations, grant writing and public speaking. Betsy serves as Public Relations Director for the New Orleans mission. Displaced by Katrina in 2005 herself, she and Bob relocated to Covington. Their daughter and husband with three children live in Australia. She and Bob are active in their local church and have served as home cell pastors since 1984. An inspirational speaker, she has organized community wide prayer efforts, led in marketplace ministry as a bible teacher at home and at work. Presently she serves as the Stonecroft Regional Administrator for Louisiana which encompasses support and encouragement for eight local volunteer groups in New Orleans and Baton Rouge.

"SHELTER has enhanced the way I think and pray about the ways God gives us protection, strength, courage, faithfulness and unconditional love. We have "shelter" as we dwell with Him. Beautifully written with warmth, one finds the writer solely committed to His everlasting love."

— PAT RUSSELL, WILMETTE, IL AND BONITA SPRINGS, FL

Board of Directors for Aging with Dignity (Five Wishes) Tallahassee,

FL Devoted volunteer, Hope Hospice Ft. Myers, FL Prayer Organizer of Midwest Presbyterian Frontier Fellowship

"For those running the race, THE SHELTER summons us to a replenishing place of pause – to reflect on the beauty of the Lord, to consider the pace and progress of our own journeys, and to contemplate our role these days as followers of Jesus. Through her reflections, Billie Cash provides a fresh seedbed for the pursuit of God with abandoned obedience – the very heart of what is necessary to change a nation."

— DAVE BUEHRING, FRANKLIN, TN

Founder and Team Leader, Lionshare Leadership Group www.lionshare.org

"In the troubling, uncertain days in which we are living, we need encouragement, direction and hope. Billie has given us all of these and more in her book THE SHELTER. With her unique style and eloquent mastery of words she draws us to the ONE who is our shelter and challenges us to be ever watchful as the day of His appearing draws near."

— PAT THOMAS, BYHALIA, MS

Free lance writer, Bible study Leader, former business entrepreneur, Pat contributed to Making The Blue Plate Special *by Florence Littauer, Marita Littauer and Lauren Littauer Briggs. She serves with the Women's Board at Central Church, Christian Writers Circle and Christian Writers Association nationally. She writes for the church newsletter and online devotional site. She is married to Larry. They have two adult children and two grandchildren. She maintains her devotional blog, www.wingsofthemornblogspot.com, with refreshing insight.*

"Billie Cash has done it again. Her observations about life and faith are those which all of us should appreciate. How many of us see God...every day. Billie...reminds us to discover God's Shelter."

— NANCY FETTERMAN, PENSACOLA, FL MA,

University of West Florida, advisor on several local and state boards; Presently, she is a Trustee for the University of West Florida, Pensacola, FL

"In *THE SHELTER*, your words have pressed me...to claim my post, to take my watch, to engage the world that surrounds by living in the Word where true freedom and life are found.... We must take a stand and hold fast to the truth we have in JESUS! It is a joy to have you cheer and spur me on in my walk with Him. Your words are written with beautiful imagery and description. I have felt invited into your experiences with you as though I was a guest in your home."

— KAITLIN ROSE, BLACKSBURG, VA

She and her husband serve in the ministry of Campus Outreach at Virginia Tech College mentoring students in leadership, character development and relationship with Christ.

"THE SHELTER is a timeless reminder that we stand in God's presence as a country, as a church, as a family and as an individual in the privacy of our own hearts. Oh, to have God cognizance each day! Having spent time reading THE SHELTER and being mentored by you this month, Billie, I have a renewed desire to passionately abide in His strength — in the shelter of His arms, in His Word, in His presence. I yearn for a mentoring faith that will reproduce His legacy from generation to generation…. In the shelter of His presence there is safety, nourishment, joy, peace, rest. Many lives will be touched by this book and turned toward the Lord. May our country experience the real *change* that is everlasting."

— Rebecca Williamson, Oxford NC

Wife, mother, mentor

"No matter where we are in life, we need a shelter. The storms of conflict, loneliness and confusion exist. In *THE SHELTER* Billie inspires us to find the One who will guide us through all turmoil to His shelter where we find peace, rest and strength."

— Wendy Wright President, Concerned Women for America, Washington, DC

An advocate for pro-family and pro-life issues, ethical policies at the United Nations, she has trained grass roots activists. Her commitment to a pro-family agenda launched freedom of speech and religion cases before the US Supreme Court, Texas Supreme Court and Florida Supreme Court. She taught at the Foursquare Bible College in Sri Lanka, trained pro-family leaders in Mexico and advised Kosovo's new government on their constitution. A frequent guest of the national media, she also writes editorials and articles for publications like USA Today, Washington Post, Atlanta Journal-Constitution, Washington Times, Human Events *and other outlets. Wendy was named among "The Most Powerful Women in Washington" in 2006 by the Washingtonian Magazine. She was recognized for her "continuous leadership in the cause of life" by The National Pro-Life Religious Council.*

"*The Shelter* is the most powerful and penetrating of Billie's writings. All my emotions were engaged – from silent tears to spontaneous laughter. Practical, inspiring principles encourage us to face any circumstance but remind us to rejoice every day as well. *Shelter* feeds the soul. Billie has lived it. Sharing it woos us to God. If you know her, you know she leaves behind the signature of God."

— AUDREY MCCLUNG, PHOENIX, AZ

Stonecroft Regional Administrator, Stonecroft Ministries; Inspirational speaker, wife to Lonny; Mother to Kim and Kurt, and Nana to four beloved grandchildren

How great is your goodness, which you have stored up for those who fear you,
Which you bestow in the sight of men on those who take refuge in you.
In the shelter of your presence you hide them from the intrigues of men.

PSALM 31:19-20A

ACKNOWLEDGEMENTS

Praying Friends, your covering over me has spurred me on in days of weakness and breakthrough as I have earnestly sought to write to the challenges we face today.

Thank you, beloved prayer group in Collierville: Ann, Denise, Pat and Joyce. You know the pressures that surround my family and I am grateful for your faithfulness.

A special thanks to my inner circle of prayer – Kate, Beth, Audrey, Marie, Peggy, Hope and Stephanie. Indeed you are a part of my prayer shelter forever.

I am grateful to all who read my manuscript and made suggestions and comments; Pat Thomas, Pat Russell.

My blessing to all who are on my internet base all over the world. You always respond when prayer alerts go out and I thank you.

The Galilean Bible Class in our church is a home to us now. You have been so faithful in prayer.

Always, my beloved husband Roy is the final edit and he is a master at it. My gratitude goes to my publishers, godly men of integrity, Sam and Tim Lowry.

In weakness, I have laid bare my weight of warning over our nation.

In strength, I have discovered the wonder of a loving God who waits for us to hear His call and return to His goodness.

In weakness, I have rediscovered the Shelter of His presence through the Word and in prayer.

In strength I have emerged to take my watch.

Thank you, Lord for giving me the charge to call your people home to THE SHELTER.

In YOUR presence is strength forevermore.

In faithfulness we will watch over our lives with expectancy and trust.

In Jesus' Name, hope is rising once again.

Billie Cash

TABLE OF CONTENTS

FOREWORD

According to a famous story, the Rev Augustus M .Toplady was walking one day through Burrington Combe, a beautiful spot in Somersetshire, England. Caught, suddenly, in a storm he was in a very exposed place and espied a massive rock beside the road in which he was able to take refuge until the storm abated.

Toplady, while in the cleft, picked up a playing card lying at his feet and wrote upon the back of it the hymn of which it has been said that, "No other English hymn can be named which has laid so broad and firm a grasp upon the English speaking world," beginning,

Rock of Ages, Cleft for me!

Let me hide myself in Thee

Walking through the beautiful conservation village of Broadhembury in Devonshire with my friend, the beloved pastor Leslie Burston, we entered the local Parish Church. There on the wall I read the following memorial inscription:

Rev. Augustus M Toplady

Vicar 1768-1778

Author of the immortal hymn, *Rock of Ages*

"To whose personal piety, brilliant gifts, sanctified learning and uncompromising advocacy of the Gospel of the Sovereign Grace of God, his writings bear abundant testimony.

Died 11th August, 1778, in his 38th year"

For by grace are ye saved through faith and that not of yourselves, it is the gift of God not of works let any man should boast.

Ephesians 2:8

Stirred deeply by what I read my eye further fell on a memorial plaque to a prominent lady of the district that was placed right beside Toplady's memorial. Part of it read,

"Her long and virtuous life was spent in the quiet and steady performance of every righteous and moral duty in humble hope of immortality"

The stark difference between the two memorials could not have been more obvious. One told of a person who died with the obvious assurance of salvation and the other told of a person who died with the mere hope of it. Was Toplady 'holier-than-thou' in his assurance of salvation? Certainly not! He noted in his immortal hymn that his salvation had nothing to do with the performance of righteous and moral duties. He wrote:

Nothing in my hand I bring
Simply to thy cross I cling;
Naked, come to Thee for dress,
Helpless look to Thee for grace;
Foul I to the fountain fly,
Wash me, Savior or I die

We are now far from those 18th century days in Broadhembury but I now find a very creative and highly gifted writer from Tennessee in the United States who in the 21st Century shelters with deep assurance exactly where Toplady sheltered – in Christ alone. In this book she describes the incredible strength she finds in that shelter for life and eternity.

The best thing about Billie's writing is that she makes me yearn to further experience that strength too. She draws me out after God, that perfect shelter in the time of storm. Having recently been diagnosed with acute myeloid leukemia I find her writing hugely pertinent. Her writing style is so lucid and unpretentious. She soars into the mystical while rooted in the practical. This book is masterpiece of devotional writing.

Billie is deeply concerned with the moral and spiritual state of her nation and from the strength she gains from God she courageously calls her nation back its biblical roots. She gently sprinkles her writing with wonderful stories of her heroes, from Harper Lee to F.B.Meyer; from Mary Slessor to C.S. Lewis. Billie has many gifts and the mastery of the short sentence is one of them. My favorite sentence points out that God may call us to the ends of the earth or to walk around the corner for him. Having spent three decades doing the first and now only able to do the second, Billie has shown me in that simple sentence that one is as important as the other. As you read this book you will, like me, often read a sentence and find it so nurturing you will be forced to set the book down and savor the sentence for a while!

Here is deep patriotism that is not fanatical. Here is love of God, family and community. Here is a book that will draw multitudes of people back to long lost precious values and more importantly back to the very heart of God.

It is a winner.

I just loved it.

Derick Bingham

Adjunct professor of English Literature, John Brown University, Siloam Springs, AR — Prolific author, teaching pastor, Christ Church, Belfast, Ireland

THE SHELTER

Abruptly I awakened to the bite of winter's prelude.

During the night a howling, frigid northern front blew through our town, dropping the temperatures to freezing for the first time. The crepe myrtle trees on our patio bowed low as a fierce rain stripped the remaining leaves, scattering them on the ground.

They were holding on to autumn's last refrain and so was I.

Sweeping gusts of wind railed against the house all night releasing mournful dissonant sounds signaling the first blast of winter. An untimely squall slammed discordant raindrops against our windows where they were easily distinguishable as the sounds of sleet.

It was the rasping, jarring rain of early winter.

Sleep became more of a dozing off and on rather than an anticipated night of languid rest.

As I lay in bed I began to pray, "Lord, you know where we are. This is our home. Protect us. We trust in YOU."

Sirens screamed through the streets as emergencies emerged.

Simultaneously the night lights in the hall flickered and then we lost electrical power. The heat ceased its cycling but the roar of nature's fury continued in movements outside.

My husband, Roy, got up to turn off the alarm system and I searched for a flashlight.

As I walked toward the kitchen I could hear the furious flapping of the flag on our front porch.

It was being whipped by a hard and determined cold rain.

After checking the house, we went back to bed and tried to settle into an unsettling night.

The power would, no doubt, be restored eventually.

It always is.

We would wait and watch until we fell asleep.

I drifted off to sleep and woke up at first light, startled by the silence.

Throughout the night we were aware of time only because of the chiming of our grandfather clock.

This beautiful stately clock, made in France for a monastery, chimes on the hour to awaken the monks to pray and then again five minutes later, as a reminder.

I love the striking sound prompting the hour.

It is a conscious cue ringing time's demand.

The tolling of time marks the measure of our days.

We each have the same amount from sunrise to sundown.

Gratefully the power was finally restored to us at 6:33am.

The day began as an overcast morning somewhat wilted from the evening's brawling deluge.

Looking outside, I noticed all the trees were now bare of all their foliage.

The American flag was limp and frayed on one corner from the night's swift lashing but she was still at her appointed post.

Traffic was resuming as people scurried to work.

School buses passed by carrying students to school.

The business of living goes on.

We had been jolted into a misty, wet chill of winter.

We somehow prefer more predicable transitions, but they are not always possible.

Storms come and storms go.

Sometimes there is a *suddenly*.

When we find ourselves in a storm we need shelter.

A storm of nature disrupts life but there are other times of stormy tumult that destroy it.

Some storms wreck our private lives.

Families fracture through divorce, abuse and addictive behavior.

Some wreck our nation.

Financial institutions fail, bringing loss to the marketplace and to our livelihood.

Some wreck the future.

Fear about provision for our legacy is real.

Some "storms" clear our minds from debris.

America is in crisis.

God is not.

HE is The Shelter and we must find our way to the Shelter every day.

Lord of the Shelter;

I am weakened from the weight of concern.

YOU are not.

I am worried for the future of generations.

YOU are not.

I am wearied over the complacency and compromise of Truth.

YOU are not.

YOU ARE TRUTH.

YOU ARE STRENGTH.

YOU ARE THE SHELTER.

Call us to our watch.

Our lives depend on it.

YOU are not asleep.

YOU are not incapacitated.

YOU are Sovereign.

We will trust in YOUR UNFAILING LOVE.

Teach us.

Train us.

Test us.

Give us YOUR PERSPECTIVE.

We will learn to live in The Shelter because YOU are there.

All storms pass.

We must live in YOUR Strength.

In obedience we bow down.

In hope we rise in Jesus' Name.

BILLIE CASH

Winter 2008

Collierville, TN

CHAPTER ONE

FINDING STRENGTH

One starts an action simply because one must do something.

— T. S. Eliot

Strength is the opposite of weakness.

My study is a place of quiet and reflection.

I draw strength by just being there.

It holds many endearing objects that remind me of my journey with God.

They put faces to my faith.

A small group of figurines reminds me of childhood: a delicately carved harp-playing angel purchased in Oberammergau, Germany; a chubby clay angel with a perpetual smile that I gave to special friends one year for Christmas; a harvest angel dressed in earth tones holding a pot of mauve mums with a spade in hand preparing to till her autumn garden, a tiny tan alabaster turtle that never moves. All these objects memorialize precious time spent with people I love.

There are photographs of grandchildren, baby pictures of my own children, Kellye and Carey, favorite duo snapshots of

Kellye, Carey, my sister Judy and me taken in special moments I want to remember. There is an antique clock forever ticking the minutes of the day and the night and a vintage photo of my mother, Frances, and her sister Peggy nearby along with a small grouping of dolls. One is a fair-haired beauty dressed in red, white and blue. She was a birthday gift from my delightful doll collector friend Stephanie. To me, the doll represents America.

My clock chimes the urgency of the hour daily and makes me aware that I am in the fourth quarter of living. The other three quarters seem to have evaporated without warning.

All around me are books: antique books, resource books of every kind, favorite authors, biographies, novels, devotionals, dictionaries, thesauruses, family Bibles and my Bibles. I have lived in books most of my life. They are friends. It is a world in which I am at home.

When I look up from my desk I read these framed words exquisitely done in calligraphy:

O Lord thou didst strike my heart with thy word and I loved Thee.

— St. Augustine

In this statement I see my calling, which is to impart the beauty, security, privilege of the love of God found in His Word and the stirring challenge to woo others to live it out intentionally every day.

And I, too, am charged to do so again and again.

I have a comfort corner in my study where there is a collection of three individual paintings of trees. These were given to me at different times of my life and now they seem to flow together as a progressive declaration of strength to me.

One canvas is a street painter's offering of a snowy Parkside scene in New York City. Tall buildings checkered with windows rise up and seem to buffet one another. In the background looms the iconic Hotel Essex. Its prominent red sign looks welcoming while inside, the rooms are lighted. The landscape reveals snow surrounding a small body of water, packed down snow that has been there for a time and a present fresh falling snow. A woman dressed in a deep comforting sea-blue coat and boots is walking by the waterside. She is holding a black umbrella as a shield to ward off the chill of the wind as snowflakes continue to fall all around her and collect on top. One senses movement in this scene. Most prevalent is a single tall tree positioned in the foreground. It is apparently in the throes of early winter for the top half has been "deleafed." There are only branches now scattered with snow. The bottom half, however, is still clinging to weathered clusters of leaves in shades of warm butter and a faint rose hue…colors found in vintage pillow cases. It is a striking montage of the true transition from autumn into winter.

My dear friend Peggy purchased the painting while on a shopping trip to New York City with her daughters and then gave it to me one year as a gift. She always meant to have it framed. It leaned against the lamp in her study for a couple of years. I would come for a visit, see it and remark to her that I really liked it. One day, it became mine when she said, "Happy birthday." The art piece found a home on the wall in my study. One day a telephone call came from a close mutual friend to tell me the sad news that Peggy had cancer. It was then that her battle with cancer for three and one half years became mine as well. I went to my post in prayer day by day keeping watch over my friend's journey of faith. As her body weakened, her faith flourished and all who knew her were strengthened as well. So many times we planned to spend a weekend in New York City together but we never made it.

To me this wonderful piece communicates the insight that a tree can be barren and beautiful at the same time...a rite of passage.

The second painting is an artistic impression of autumn which my mother had in her den with a group of what she called "happy scenes." Mae Sibley was a local artist from Memphis in the 1960's who highlighted bright background colors which easily set apart the objects to be painted. This small canvas is splashed with a startling yellow sky muted here and there and intense in other areas. Small birds are in the distance as is a country planked fence. The scene is cast in a field in the autumn with blowing grasses in shades of pale wheat scattered with patches of penny brown. Once again a tree in the forefront captures the focus. It is plush and overflowing with rich, mellowing apricot leaves tinged with garnet burnished copper on every branch, a beauty to behold. A diminutive companion tree is lodged in the distance. It is round and bushy by design but is also heavily laden with lush leaves of beaten burgundy.

To me, this work of art stands as a perpetual interpretation of the blaze of autumn.

In the year of my mother's death, my watch over her illness took my strength but I was aware that my God was keeping watch over me. "The happy scenes" we reflect upon daily are a choice, a reminder of the constancy of God's love. As Mother became weakened in body, her faith swelled with strength and infused her life with hope eternal and the promise of heaven's glory. Mother's autumn will forever remain as beautifully timeless as this painting.

A tree is a creation of God. Each season portrays dimensions of life.

The last artistic rendering in this triad of tree art has become the encapsulation of my faith journey for this book.

This memento was sent to me during the most arduous year of my life by my ever caring friend Hope. Within two months of the fall of 2007, I lost my closest confidante Peggy and my mother Frances. The loss brought exhaustion.

I wrote about it in my book, *A Pillow on the Highway*.

Loss also creates weakness.

What is planted in our lives springs to the surface while we are hanging on. This powerfully graphic work by Jaye Williamson is done in black and white. A mature tree of enormous proportion dominates the starkly riveting scene. The landscape is dwarfed by its existence, making it hard to distinguish other plantings. They don't seem to matter. The tree's branches are like massive tentacles twisting upward and reconfiguring themselves to allow space for the open sky. It is a giant embrace, a presence. Spindly tall trees and scruffy shapeless ones flank it, interspersed all around by dense underbrush. An obscure mountain to the left is hidden by other trees. The clouds, like puffs of gray smoke, encircle it. A worn out gate is nearby and the roof of a home is barely visible, but it is there. At first look I was caught up by a forlorn sadness for there was no obvious beauty.

The tree is bare.

It has been denuded, stripped.

No leaves,

No color,

No snow,

No people,

But there it is, present, living, established as though it is standing watch.

When I read the title *Shelter of Strength* I knew the direction of this book.

Today I am at my post writing and keeping watch.

My study is a shelter of my own orchestration, for I am surrounded by treasures of remembrance.

It is a place of refuge.

I walk in, sit, think and then open my heart to my Lord, earnestly seeking His guidance in how to live in this moment.

I experience peace here and am strengthened but I was not meant to live in my study,

Neither are you.

The vineyard of America is suffering from root rot.

It needs tending.

The walls of liberty and justice are caving.

To live with today's uncertainty we must find the Shelter of God's Presence day and night.

When we live there, our faith will be fortified and we will be strengthened to keep watch.

God's strength is a HOPE unwavering, everlasting, indestructible.

The colossal leafless tree stands as a sentinel of limitless potential, a shelter of strength.

The weight of warning is upon us.

The watch of vigilance is a siren of alert.

These words dictate the dilemma:

> I understand by 'freedom of spirit' something quite definite — the unconditional will to say "No" where it is dangerous to say no.

— Nietzsche

We may have to learn to say no.

We must consciously revive virtue.

We must nurture character.

We must dig up the fallow ground of falsehood and ditch the weeds that sabotage the blooms of faith providing space for fresh growth.

We can, if we will live in integrity and godliness.

God is calling us to be watchmen.

My trinity of tree portraits reveals Truth.

Trees persevere through the seasons for they have a rooted network spiraling out from their base, providing stability.

Barren or beautiful, they are still trees.

They endure and so must we.

To do so we must keep watch over our lives and our land.

From heaven, Yahweh looks down and sees all men and watches the inhabitants of earth. Because of Him, no army saves a ruler; but the eyes of the Lord watch those who fear Him and He delivers them from death, famine and lost hope.[1]

God has a watch.

Living outside His shelter isn't wise.

He knew we would need access to the Shelter so Jesus came, birthing belonging and intimacy through the CROSS.

Anyone can come.

The Bible records Jesus' death, burial and resurrection.

It fosters the timeless search we all have for a relationship to a God of love who forgives our wayward minds, our reckless depravity and invites us each to sit at His table.

Sin suffocates.

Love liberates.

Weakness wanes.

Strength secures.

Receive, believe and stand at your post....

How great is your goodness which you have stored up for those who fear you, which you bestow in the sight of men who take refuge in you. In the SHELTER of YOUR PRESENCE you hide them from the intrigues of men, in your dwelling you keep them safe.[2]

Come to the Shelter!

Find His strength.

God's children go "from strength to strength"[3]

Are you one of them?

A WATCHFUL EYE

1. Why do I run from facing my own weakness?
2. Does God have a plan for me?
3. Can I learn to live in the Shelter of His Presence?

WATCHWORD
Courage is not simply one of the virtues, but the form of every virtue at the testing point.

— C. S. Lewis

PRAYER WATCH

Faithful Father;

I come.

I am weak.

My shallow choices have choked the life of my soul.

It is dry and brittle.

I have pursued a restless way saturated with momentary pleasures.

More of anything is not what I need.

More of YOU I plead.

I am filled with fear over the crisis in my nation.

Nothing is secure.

I watch the news and see no end to the losses that are coming.

I am worried about my job, my family, my forever.

My dreams are vanishing before my eyes.

I am losing ground.

I have wasted years in pursuit of grasping, unworthy ambitions.

Now I can believe that YOU have patiently waited for me to come to the end of myself.

I am there.

Jesus, I come.

Accept me now, weak and broken.

Cleanse me from sin and wash away the debris of my debt and doubt.

Forgive me.

I come to the Shelter of YOUR LOVE.

I will purpose to live there.

I know YOU will provide.

I will take up my watch and care for others.

I now belong to YOU.

With expectancy and hope I bow down and pray in YOUR NAME.

Today the barren became beautiful because I am YOURS.

CHAPTER TWO

A SUMMONS TO WATCH

When the fight begins within himself, a man's worth something.

— Robert Browning

When I am weak, I am strong.[1]

How can that be?

We know weakness comes but how can we be strong in weakness?

Worry weakens.

Sloth weakens.

Hunger weakens.

Selfishness weakens.

When a society begins to collapse, we begin to question, to internalize anxiety and when we do, we get weak.

Mentoring stories of faith found in God's Word will help to develop within us *God cognizance* in the midst of our weakness.

What is it?

The word *cognizance* embodies knowledge, familiarity, discernment, awareness, consciousness, insight, perception, watchfulness.

To have this we must live in the Word of God. When we do so, we become a people who comprehend change with a sensitive spiritual discernment. We then find supernatural guidance in scripture which equips us to live.

God dwells in His Word.

How?

Author Eugene Peterson comments, "Christians feed on scripture. Holy Scripture nurtures...we don't simply learn or study or use scripture; we assimilate it, take into our lives in such a way that it gets metabolized into acts of love, cups of cold water...healing...justice in Jesus' Name."

The Word of God establishes stability and a holy expectancy within us.

Living in His Word transforms us daily.

Always, we are answering the question in one direction or the other: *Will we live with God, or without God? Ours is a "with God" life and we must choose: God is with us – will we be with God?* [2]

We need embedded faith.

This is *Life with God*.

The Paul of scripture with astute insight recorded these words for us:

To keep me from becoming conceited because of these surpassing revelations, there was given me a thorn in the flesh.... Three times I pleaded with the Lord to take it away from me, a messenger... of torment. But he said to me, 'My grace is sufficient for you for my power is made perfect in weakness.' Therefore I will more gladly boast about my weaknesses so that Christ's power may rest upon me. That is why for Christ's sake, I delight in weaknesses, in insults, in hardships, in persecutions, in difficulties. For when I am weak I am strong. [3]

Paul's intelligence, privileged background and scholarship were solid facts.

He could have just settled in to this known reality because it was his,

But a loving omnipotent God had been watching with other plans in mind.

He knew inside Paul was a man who could stand against the world of hatred because he had known it.

He had lived there.

Saul of Tarsus, the rampaging tyrant who hated Christ followers and tortured them, was to become Paul, a Christ Bearer, and many would join him.

Almighty God arranged for the dramatic encounter that would blind him physically.

Saul was on his way to Damascus to arrest any Christians who might be found in synagogues.

Plotting ideas in his head, suddenly he was accosted by a strange unexpected light which forced him to the ground.

He then heard a voice, "*Saul, Saul why do you persecute me?*" [4]

He answered "*Who are you, Lord?*" [5]

"*I am Jesus whom you are persecuting. Go now into Damascus and you will be told what to do.*" [6]

This was a personal summons from God Himself.

He spoke to Saul.

Can you imagine?

The shock itself would have been disabling and, in fact, when he stood up he realized he was sightless. Saul had to be led into the city. For three days he remained blind. In fact, he ate no food and drank no water.

Saul was forced into a fast from life as he knew it to be.

A messenger named Ananias was summoned in a dream to go to and touch him with healing. Filled with remorse for his error, his sin, his drivenness to destroy believers, Saul embraced the Life of Christ. He was forgiven and sight was restored.

One can be a sincere zealot and be sincerely misguided.

With this conversion experience, his name was changed to Paul and the world of Christianity exploded.

If Paul had not surrendered to Christ "we would be missing thirteen of twenty seven books of the New Testament and Christianity's early major expansion...." [7]

He moved from self centered independence to God dependence and then into interdependence with his brothers and sisters.

He would be known as Paul the apostle.

His perspective was richly expounded for now he had God cognizance.

The events of his life were viewed through the lens of grace magnified in Christ Jesus.

His seared conscience was replete now with transparent understanding, for his heavenly Father had found him, healed him and summoned him.

All his training, knowledge and talent now merged into a leadership dynamic.

He understood that inflated arrogance is not acceptable to God. The scripture uses the word "conceit". To keep him from conceit because of his extraordinary ability, Paul's thorn in the flesh was given to him and was not removed. Repeatedly he asked for relief and in the denial of this request he discovered the goodness and greatness of God's grace. This thorn of weakness imbued him with the strength of God.

"Throughout history, the letters of Paul, with the rest of scripture, have been threatened with destruction. But no force has proved able to destroy what God deems indestructible…. Curious isn't it? God stopped a man who was carrying letters of authority to destroy the church, and then He inspired that same man to write letters that would strengthen the church." [8]

When he was weak he was strong.

The living principle of "being made perfect in weakness" is a life of deliberate dependency upon the Divine One who knows our weakness and knows how His power will be given to us in it.

The boast of Paul's life changed course.

He would revel in the sufficiency of a God ordained life for his devotion would be in Christ alone.

The God of the Word has always provided strength for His children.

Summon your power, O God. Show us your strength, O God as you have done before. [9]

There will be strength for today and strength for tomorrow.

Paul's determined resolve to follow Christ brought forth hardships in the form of beatings, misrepresentations, imprisonments and even shipwreck.

The days of persecution for him would descend and scripture confirms it.

You, however, know all about my teaching, my way of life, my purpose, faith, patience, love endurance, persecutions, sufferings…yet the Lord rescued me from all of them. In fact, everyone who wants to live a godly life in Christ Jesus will be persecuted. [10]

What did he mean by rescue?

He did suffer.

Is suffering a rescue?

God's rescue is the empowering given to those who have learned to live in the Shelter of His Presence.

Enemies around Paul raged against his new faith in Christ. Resistance constantly met him but he stood for truth and believing God would be with him.

And He was.

But the Lord stood at my side and gave me strength....[11]

The Light of Christ had pierced his darkness with purpose.

Paul was given an assignment, a post,

And so are we.

For thus has the Lord said unto me: go set (yourself as) a watchman on the wall. Let him declare what he sees.[12]

Does God call *us* to watch?

He does.

Will we be tested?

We will.

Can we live with confidence in His provision?

We can.

The summons is here and now.

Men and women who live in the Shelter of His Presence know how to live.

The walls of our nation have broken down because we have opted for an expedient self-absorbed life, abandoning the admonitions, instructions and promises of scripture.

Life with God is about God.

Biblical history points the way to rebuild what has been destroyed.

The wall of Jerusalem was also broken down and in desperate need of repair.

As we step into the Bible again and listen for God's voice speaking to His people, He calls out another watchman to lead.

This time it is Nehemiah, the Cupbearer to King Artaxerxes of Persia.

In modern terminology, Nehemiah was the chief of staff.

Specifically, the role of cupbearer was to taste the wine before the king partook of it.

Since it was not uncommon for kings to be poisoned, the one chosen for this position was highly regarded and many times endeared. Trust and loyalty were desirable attributes for the cupbearer.

Nehemiah displayed these qualities.

If, indeed, the wine was tainted unto death the cupbearer would die first sparing the king's life.

King Artaxerxes employed this ardent man of God who lived for God.

The story launches when Nehemiah encounters Hanani, a brother from Judah. He inquires about the well-being of the Jewish remnant that had survived the exile. The response was devastating.

Those who survived the exile and are back in the province are in great trouble and disgrace. The wall of Jerusalem is broken down and its gates have been burned with fire.[13]

Imagine hearing the news that your homeland is in ruins.

What should be the response when disastrous news comes?

Are there biblical models to emulate?

Can we learn from them?

We can.

We must.

Nehemiah exhibited a life integrated and transfixed with the spiritual disciplines of prayer and fasting, obedience and service.

He was not blindsided.

He did not have to have a refresher course in Faith 101.

His Life with God was not in crisis.

In an instant Nehemiah translated the anguish he felt into a cry to God.

"O Lord God of heaven, the great and awesome God, who keeps his covenant of love with those who love him and obey his commands, let your ear be attentive and your eyes open to hear the prayer your servant is praying before you day and night for your servants." [14]

Chapter One of Nehemiah flows with a heart for prevailing prayer, conscious confession of sin, an earnest call for his errant people to return to the God he loved. He pleaded for a people "whom you redeemed by your great strength and your mighty hand." [15]

This man of God wept over the destruction of the city wall and he repented for the sins of generations who had allowed this to happen.

God heard and prepared the king's heart to give favor to Nehemiah's request.

Permission was granted for him to travel to his people.

His summons was obtained.

Letters of introductions for safe conduct and supplies needed were appropriated.

And because the gracious hand of my God was upon me the king granted my requests. [16]

Upon arriving in Jerusalem he surveyed the damage under cover of darkness with a few men.

They examined the walls and the gates carefully.

He did his homework.

Jerusalem lies in ruins and its gates have been burned with fire. Come let us rebuild the wall and we will no longer be in disgrace. The God of heaven will give us success. We his servants will start rebuilding. [17]

He had confidence to believe his plan would work.

Nehemiah then organized resources, people, and monies and created a structure for the plan. He allocated time and sought expertise. Utilizing the skills of others was mandatory but he also encouraged constant dialogue amongst them as they met challenges. This was a key to implementing progress. Many leaders with their crews were recruited and worked together side by side.

The wall was just the beginning of his vision to rehabilitate the nation.

Calamities were anticipated. Feedback was earnestly solicited and when opposition came knocking he was ready with a contingency plan of prayer and action.

Sanballat and Tobiah fiercely opposed Nehemiah's plan so he called his people together and *they prayed to God and posted a guard day and night.* [18]

He knew that exhaustion, financial deficits and differences of opinion would be a constant source of ill will.

Enemies stalked every move with surveillance.

For protection he designed a strategy of stationing people behind the lowest points of the walls and posting families there with swords, spears and bows. When this was in operation he summoned the officials together and then stood up before all of the people and said, "*Don't be afraid of them. Remember the Lord is great and awesome and fight for your brothers, your sons and daughters, your wives and your homes.*" [19]

Enemies then backed off.

Work resumed and from that day on half of the men did the work while the other half kept an armed watch. There were guards by night and workmen by day.

A man with a trumpet kept vigil beside Nehemiah.

When you hear the sound of the trumpet, join there. Our God will fight for us! [20]

There were assaults ahead to halt the progress through malicious slander, false reports and ruthless intimidation but prayer for strength continued and so did the work.

I prayed, now strengthen my hands.[21]

The wall was completed in fifty two days.

When our enemies heard about this they were afraid and lost confidence because they realized this work had been done with the help of our God.[22]

Nehemiah took his watch and was rewarded.

Will we be?

Are we running from the watch God intends?

It was September of 2008 and I found myself on the campus of the University of Mississippi involved in an event called *Issues Alley*. It had been organized to promote the first Presidential

Debate of the campaign season which would be held there and televised throughout the world. The world was watching and so was God. This was an election year in America. *Issues Alley* was a conglomeration of invited groups, vendors, organizations and media. They would represent the diverse spectrum of interests that could be found on a college campus.

I had not planned to go, but God had.

He frequently positions people in our lives that will lead us to the next plateau of commitment to Him.

Sometimes we follow and sometimes we do not.

These folks bear His image.

He placed one of them before me.

My friend Norma is a refined, genteel lady with a tenacious God cognizance.

She is fidelity activated.

Norma had been contacted a few days before the event by *Concerned Women for America*, an organization she knows well for she has been involved with it for over thirty years. College organizers had contacted them and asked them to send some representation. With short notice she was to make preparations for a booth which would be a part of the event.

Immediately, Norma began to pray for two women to go with her and apparently I was to be one of them. She then sent out an e-mail presenting the opportunity. It was short on notice but far reaching in passion.

I pondered it and then did some inquiry about the organization. The mission statement of *Concerned Women for America is* "To protect and promote Biblical values among all citizens – first through prayer, then education, finally by influencing our society, thereby reversing the decline in moral values in our nation."

I was drawn when I read it.

As I began to pray about going, I tried to rationalize my way out because I really was not a bona fide member of this group.

But I was deeply burdened about the God void in our culture and as I consciously looked for a way to decline, the God who watches would not let me opt out.

I knew God's plan was for me to go.

Early in the morning of September 26, 2008, Norma, accompanied by her dear husband Bob, drove to pick up Sandra, the other chosen, scrappy cohort and me, and off to Oxford, Mississippi we went. In southern vernacular, we left at "O-dark thirty."

The crispness of an early autumn day greeted us but was short lived, for by afternoon Indian summer temperatures swelled humidity and sane thinking began to evaporate.

A prayer alert had gone out the night before to many that God might give us utterance, opportunity and protection.

He did.

We were the first ones to arrive and set up in The Grove. While Sandra and Norma tweaked our table with brochures and positioned the materials, I felt led to prayer walk the area. By 9 am some booths were assembling. A live band was tuning up with stage and screen supplied. Political booths were in progress for both national parties. Organized efforts were underway for a variety of food vendors. Then stations for computers, cell phones, voter registration and the media followed. As I walked and prayed, I sensed a stealth foreboding shadowing me. At first I could not define it. Returning to our booth I talked with Norma and Sandra as we prepared to share ideas with those we would engage. Our booth had an easel holding a replica of the Constitution, the founding document of our nation and the literature on the table substantiated the Word of God as the authority on family issues such as protecting the life of the unborn and the support of the definition of marriage.

So we were a patriotic God booth.

By eleven o'clock the tension of the day popped. The band revved up accompanied by an energetic choir that sang everything from rock to Gospel. They began to sway and saturate the afternoon with reeling rhythms that escalated into increasingly strident levels of sound. After awhile the words were obscured and the beat took over, rendering a happening filled with sound and fury and signifying…little. The music dominated. Eventually its backdrop of demanding dissonance made conversation almost impossible. It became hard to hear and hard to speak, a toll defusing clarity needed in communication.

This event was supposed to be an opportunity for all of us to speak with one another about concerns and issues.

Like a beehive, The Grove was soon alive with activity and other booths were added to round out the assemblage. There were advocates for alternative energy, affordable tuition, justice for human rights in Darfur, AIDS education and research, women's rights, civil rights, war protesters, troop support, poverty, climate and many organizations targeting a specific issue.

Lunchtime found me scouting around visiting the last booths to set up. I made a concerted effort to speak to those who were manning them. I diligently searched to see if there were any religious organizations on campus that might be overtly represented.

Faith is a voice.

I am sure there were reasons why I found none.

But it was a startling moment when I realized our booth was it…the token.

We knew we were there to bring God's presence into this arena.

Now I understood what I had sensed in the prayer walk, the stifling oppression.

Solo does not mean alone.

Sometimes it means significant.

Soon tee shirts, bumper stickers and placards abounded everywhere and we were inundated with college students, reporters or firebrand, periphery folks who came to share their one issue.

I recognized in standing for biblical values and the constitution, our position might also be viewed as extreme.

So be it.

It is a risk I now must take.

That steamy, sweltering day on a college campus captured a culture gone far afield from righteousness.

I studied faces and earnestly listened as young women who needed mothering came by. I watched Sandra gently take the hand of two young men and talk to both of them about God's love and plan for their lives. She spoke to them about consequences and they received what she said because her life exuded the peace His Life imparts when we are centered in Him. Sandra was well acquainted with their issues. Her voice resonated truth. We had so many encounters that day. There were teachers who wanted flyers to use in presentations in school, professors casting a disparaging eye as they passed by, television personalities who were thankful there was only one booth like us and once in a while someone stopped and said, "Thanks for being here."

There was a watershed moment in which I was singled out for dialogue. An inquisitive young fellow apparently usually adept in disarming his critics approached me. He wanted to know what I felt about war and poverty. I referenced that in the Bible we are reminded that there will be wars and rumors of war (Matthew 24:6-7). War would always be a reality somewhere. Then I shared that according to the Bible the poor would always be with us (Mark 14:7). So indeed we would forever be tasked with resolving these issues.

Fervently praying within I continued, "No elected official will ever eradicate war and poverty from the world." He winced.

Then I spoke about believing in the Sovereignty of God.

That statement was a fuse, igniting condescending laughter meant to mock me.

He was patronizingly jocular at the presumption of my faith.

Steeliness crept into me and I responded, "Do not demean me if you expect to have discussion."

He fell quiet for an instant. It was as if a switch had flipped.

But gathering himself once again he sneeringly added, "So since I believe war is sin, then God must make us sin because he is sovereign, right?"

"No," I replied, "God does not make us sin but He knows we are going to sin. He always knows what's coming. He will have the last word."

In effect he had tried to present a disdainful, distorted view of God.

I countered, "America is the land of the free but *my* world view is Christian."

His was not so we were stalemated. My final statement was this: "Son, you are in your twenties and I am in my sixties. Our military career of thirty years moved me to cry out to God for help. I had to learn how to live and raise children with a husband who was gone in defense of this nation. I found the answer in God's Word. It works. It is Truth. I am not alone. There are thousands of people like me who also have learned to live in it. We will not be silent. We will vote, live and serve from a biblical conscience. We are not retreating. Good day."

At that moment I experienced a sinking, physical weakness.

I was faint.

Needing to take a break after this volatile discourse, I walked over to the Law Centre across the street for it had been assigned as the spot to go for breaks. There were comfortable, overstuffed chairs and sofas, restrooms and snack machines. I collapsed into the first chair I saw for a momentary breather but got no relief until I got down on my knees and cried out to God for strength. Waves of grief swept over me. I came into the Shelter of His Presence. The weight of warning was upon me.

I wept unashamedly.

I was shaken to the core of my being.

After several moments I stood up resolute and walked back to my post.

I purposed to continue.

Confusion, strife, clamor, scorn are voices of deception.

We carry the Life of Christ.

I wanted to repair the walls of my land.

God had to stretch me.

The road to Oxford changed my watch.

I can never go back to comfortable Christianity.

A passive faith is past.

Embedded faith is aware of God's Watch.

The Bible equips us to read the news and identify who, what, where and how and then to be compelled to participate.

We are supposed to be consciously engaged in the world in which we live.

Viewing the events surrounding our lives with God cognizance will bring discernment.

Rebuilding is a team effort.

When I returned home I was spent,

But God was not.

He who refreshes others will himself be refreshed.[23]

I have now expanded my watch.

"God's primary call, his address to us always has dimensions: summons and invitation, law and grace, demand and offer.... Disciples are not so much those who follow as those who *must* follow."[24]

The summons now is upon you.

Come to the Shelter.

Find strength.

Be refreshed.

Your post is waiting.

A WATCHFUL EYE

1. How can your weakness be used to strengthen you?

2. Have you been stretched to go to a new place in your faith?

3. Is there a wall you need to rebuild in your home, in your community, in your nation?

WATCHWORD
The acknowledgement of our weakness is the first step in repairing our loss.

—Thomas A Kempis

PRAYER WATCH

Ever Watchful Father;

How well YOU understand weakness.

Our lives are meant to be in partnership with YOU.

We are enticed to travel down many roads.

Coming to the intersection of faith forces us to decide which way we will go.

A fork in the road requires decision.

We either choose Life with YOU or we choose Life without YOU.

Not choosing is a choice.

YOUR Word has been given to us as a map, a guide.

We can live between its pages as men and women of other generations have done and in so doing be continually transformed or we can choose to listen to other voices which deny faith.

A pattern for living unfolds as we seek YOU daily but sometimes we simply step away from what we know in exchange for what we don't know and when we do...we become weak.

Detours can rob us of peace and possibility for we never arrive at the destination we seek.

Finding our way back to YOU is the road to faith.

YOU have never abandoned us for YOU are always watching.

Our religious liberties were given to us when our nation was founded.

Men and women came here to worship YOU in spirit and in truth.

They were a people who revered the Bible and followed its teachings.

We repent for we have lost our way to YOU.

Summon us home to the Word.

Lead us to our watch.

Living In the Word we will live.

CHAPTER THREE

BEAUTY WATCH

Though we travel the world over to find the beautiful, we must carry it with us or we find it not.

— Ralph Waldo Emerson

Beauty strengthens.

Categories of beauty are multi dimensional but universal.

Beauty has elements of design, form and color.

Why do we hunger for beauty?

Where do we go to find it?

What do we do with it?

Art has always provided insight into our desire for beauty. Galleries are filled with treasures for the mind because art makes one think. Great painters have left behind much to muse.

Beauty strengthens.

The art of nature is inviting and I relish my time spent in its midst. It too is invigorating for it flows with simplicity from beauty born from being itself...nature. In seasons it shouts to us in broad artistic strokes of hue, movement, inertia and clarity. The serene tranquility of Sparks Lake in the Oregon Cascades is captured by photographer Ric Ergenbright in such stillness that it becomes a mirror for the snow capped mountain surrounded by tall staggered pines in the distance. It is as if there was an upside down photograph in the lake. In his pictorial work, *The Art of God* our minds enter nature's beauty of dissimilarity. A completely opposite energy reigns as one observes the advancing rapids cascading over a mighty rock held hostage in the Chujenzi River in Japan. It presents an unending eternal rush. A dazzling desert sunrise in Monument Valley, Utah awakens the horizon to the day as rock formations replicating a ghost town are shrouded in shadows until the precise moment the sun lifts its morning face up over a ridge exploding fiery ribbons of golden light into tangerine trails. It is a canvas prepared in the heavens for eyes which open at dawn to embrace. Sunset in Big Sur, California finds the ocean's graying swells sweeping languidly along the coastline carrying with it the promise of constancy as the sun prepares for the end of another day. The ocean remains majestic in its own beauty.

Waters, mountains, deserts, light and darkness speak of The Artist Creator who gives us glorious glimpses of beauty.

Strength and beauty are in his sanctuary.[1]

God has placed them before us to draw us to Himself. He sets the boundaries and seasons.

You have set the boundaries of the earth; you have made summer and winter.[2]

God orchestrates nature.

The sun rises and the sun sets and hurries back to where it rises. The wind blows to the south and turns to the north; round and round it goes, ever returning on its course. All streams flow to the sea, yet the sea is never full. To the place the streams come from, there they return again.[3]

He draws us to beauty.

Nature is His art.

In it we learn about ourselves.

In contemplating and executing a work of art, the artist pours himself into communicating what he believes about significance. His work is a reflection of time, place, behavior, adornment, perspective and yes, beauty. He teaches us to consider life experience. Sometimes we find we must return to where we began or purpose to go back to the wrong turn in the road where we got diverted. Most importantly there is a bidding to constantly review where we are going every day.

Even going nowhere is somewhere.

Destination matters.

This discovery has caused me to seek after the beauty of God and discover His perspective.

Art reveals it.

In Henri Nowen's book *The Return of the Prodigal Son*, God's Hand of grace draws the reader into conclusions which will affect life lessons. It is unique because it is not only written passionately by an accomplished man possessing God cognizance but the book is centered around the notable painting by Rembrandt also entitled *The Return of the Prodigal Son*. Therefore we have an unusual weaving of an author's work and a painter's offering enveloped into one entity.

Nouwen was drawn to study this painting after having seen a poster of it a few years earlier. He had returned from an exhausting lecture tour abroad and when he happened to stumble upon it in a friend's office it caused him to pause and ponder. What he saw in the poster was the homecoming of a son lovingly embraced by a caring father. It spoke to his weariness but went deeper into his relationship with God for it represented an "ongoing yearning of the human spirit, the yearning for a final return, an unambiguous sense of safety, a lasting home." [4] The painting embodied a personal spiritual quest for Henri Nouwen.

It also revealed Rembrandt's search.

He had torments as many artists do and one of his critics Paul Baudiquet said "Since his youth, Rembrandt has but one vocation: to grow old." It seemed to be true for he was drawn by what he perceived as the inner beauty in the aged. Then he became fascinated by the blind. It is said that his most gripping portraits were done in the later years. The partially blind Simeon was a subject in one of them. The message we receive about Rembrandt is this: As his personal life began to wane and diminish "he comes in touch with the immense beauty of the interior life." [5]

The pursuit of ambition, money and adulation does wane.

What does Rembrandt's painting convey?

Predominant in the foreground of it is the half blind father wearing a deep crimson cloak standing with his hands completely out stretched pulling his son to him.

He is initiating.

The spendthrift prodigal son is broken, penitent, and partially shoeless on bended knees pressing his head toward his father's bosom.

He is receiving.

There are various onlookers. One is the elder brother who seems detached yet he is present. The colors are earthy, warm and comforting. A light silhouettes the father's face. It is a scene of love and acceptance.

Where do we find this story?

Rembrandt painted a parable of amazing proportions found in the Word of God.

There was a man who had two sons. The younger son said to his father, 'Father give me my share of the estate. So he divided his property between them. Not long after that, the younger son got together all he had. Set off for a distant country and there squandered his wealth in wild living. After he had spent everything, there was a severe famine in that whole country, and he began to be in need. So he went and hired himself out as a citizen of that country, who sent him to his fields to feed pigs. He longed to fill his stomach with the pods that the pigs were eating but no one gave him anything. When he came to his senses, he said, 'How many of my father's hired men have food to spare, and here I am starving to death! I will set out and go back to my father and say to him, 'Father, I have sinned against heaven and against you. I am no longer worthy to be called your son; make me one of your hired men'. So he got up and went to his father. But while he was still a long way off, his father saw him and filled with compassion for him; he ran to his son, threw his arms around him and kissed him.[6]

The human condition is now painted for us with words from The Word.

What do we glean?

There was a father with sons who were bound by chords of love.

One son brazenly asks for his share of the family's inheritance while his father still lives.

This request represents a cold disrespect and callous disregard for his father. Surely the father's heart must have been crushed but he agrees to the terms.

With an insatiable appetite for wild living, the errant son squanders wealth and finds himself in a pig pen where his hunger forces him to remember life as it used to be in his father's house.

Awakened to his senses he starts the trek home to forgiveness.

A loving father's feeble, partially blind eyes scoured the horizon day after day yearning for this son and one day in the distance he could not believe what he saw. A question formed in his mind. Is it possible? Then he began to run as fast as he could run to embrace this bedraggled, dirty, starving son who in despair had finally returned home.

This is the story of reconciliation which is beautiful in God's sight and healing in ours but there is more.

The father said to his servants, 'Quick! Bring the best robe and put it on him. Put a ring on his finger and sandals on his feet. Bring the fatted calf and kill it. Let's have a feast and celebrate. For this son of mine was dead and is alive again; he was lost and is found.' [7]

But not everyone wanted to celebrate.

The elder brother heard the music and dancing and came home to discover that his characterless brother had the audacity to return. He was angry and would not participate in the gathering even though his father pleaded with him.

The brother's words were indicting. *'Look! All these years I've been slaving for you and never disobeyed your orders. You never gave me even a young goat so I could celebrate with my friends. But when this son of yours squandered your property with prostitutes, you kill the fatted calf for him!'* *The father answered, 'My son you are always with me and everything I have is yours. But we had to celebrate and be glad because this brother of yours was dead and is alive again; he was lost and is found.'* [8]

Oh, the ugliness in life.

Even when there is a home coming, envy and jealousy can sabotage celebration.

Joy and resentment cannot exist together.

The elder brother's perfunctory, duty bound, loveless response is not hard to understand.

What he said was true but he too was lost.

Self conscious, calculating and filled with disdain he needs to arrest the words of his father, "You are always with me and everything I have is yours."

The father reinstates a lost vagabond son and extends full affirmation to the loyal elder son.

Both need love.

Both are unique.

Both have voids.

The prodigal son's heart was filled with craving and dissatisfaction.

The dutiful son's heart was filled with pity and defense.

The father's heart was filled only with compassionate longing for he wanted to be reunited with his sons at home.

So does our Heavenly Father.

We can see ourselves in these three men.

And when we are old we will have been all of them.

Careless impulsive youth, prideful ego driven achievement and finally gracious charity coupled with gratitude liberally dispersed by one who loves completely.

According to Henri Nouwen he tells us that "the painting contained not only the heart of the story that God wants to tell me, but also the heart of the story I want to tell God and God's people. All of the gospel is there. All of my life is there. All of the lives of my friends are there. The painting has become a mysterious window through which I can step into the Kingdom of God."[9]

Strength and beauty are in his sanctuary.[10]

Forgiveness is beautiful.

I see the beauty of God in nature and artists agree for they leave it behind.

I see the beauty of God in story and art for it is written and painted.

I see the beauty of God in scripture for it presents the way to live in harmony with one another.

I have perceived He is the beauty for which I hunger.

There are beauties to captivate us every day: absorbing the spring garden filled with the gardener 's handiwork of purple velvet pansies and bouncy yellow jonquils nodding their faces in the breeze, enjoying the absolute pleasure in watching a baby wiggling his toes and exploring them because they are his, recreating beauty in a room with function and personal taste blended with elements of color and design to accentuate it, listening to the stirring power of Rachmaninoff's music or the soothing strains of Debussy, taking a brisk invigorating morning walk of inward thought and outward gaze, experiencing a quiet, cool night sky in the autumn filled with twinkling stars pleading for us to stop and look.

There is much beauty for us to see but how diligent are we in keeping watch?

Beauty strengthens.

There are paths of beauty that women pursue relentlessly.

Our society today reveals an inordinate obsession with individuality and perfection.

The fountain of youth has always had allure but now it is a compulsion.

The American Society for Aesthetic Plastic Surgery (ASEPS) reports that as of February 2008, 11.7 million men and women have had surgical cosmetic procedures. This is an increase of 457 percent since 1997. The largest group is age 35–50 at 47 percent while the youngest is 18 and under at 2 percent. This is a statistic that covers gender and ethnicity as well as age.[11]

What does this statistic say?

It says we are intent in our pursuit of looking good on the outside; i.e., perfection.

Facts reveal focus.

In the world of fashion we buy magazines filled with beautiful models who wear whatever they like and so we fantasize that we can also; i.e., individuality.

Imagine a dress form where you can add or subtract, dress or undress, drape, tie or knot fabric around it, accessorizing it with ribbon or jewelry.

The shape of the form is the platform on which you make choices.

You are the platform.

You and I get to choose.

Far away we have strayed from God's concept of beauty for women.

Our Creator knows our bodies are a composite of genes which reproduce bone structure, skin tone, the shape and color of eyes and teeth as well as the size of hands and feet.

We must accept who we are.

Tall is tall.

Short is short.

Tall can be willowy and elegant even statuesque.

Short can be diminutive and adorable even doll like.

Over weight happens.

Sometimes it is the results of choice and sometimes there are medical factors which enter requiring medicines.

To be thinner is a goal for most women even though this too can become a medical problem if it is an obsession that obliterates all balance.

We long to find for ourselves an acceptable norm.

Both extremes are exploited in the world of beauty and made a consuming pursuit for women.

What we do with what we have is our choice every day.

The platform is our body the outward woman.

A woman should know herself inside and out.

The inner life of the woman is where real beauty is born.

It is birthed in the heart.

Your beauty should not come from outward adornment, such as braided hair and the wearing of gold jewelry and fine clothes. Instead it should be that of your inner self, the unfading beauty of a gentle and quiet spirit, which is of great worth in God's sight. For this is the way holy women of the past who put their hope in God used to make themselves beautiful.[12]

This instruction does not say we cannot have braided hair, gold jewelry or fine clothes.

It tells us that our beauty is not found in them — in *outward adornment.* When we enter into relationship with God, His beauty begins as well as His available influence over our choices,

But we are the ones who choose.

How we care for our bodies which include our dress is a statement about our Life with Him.

One thing I ask of the Lord, this is what I seek that I may dwell in the house of the Lord all the days of my life, to gaze upon the beauty of the Lord and seek him in his temple.[13]

Living in His Word, loving His presence in prayer, cultivating a gentle spirit which submits to serving others with all that we are is the essence of dwelling with Him.

His beauty is shelter.

Inner beauty is godliness.

Nurturing our spiritual lives first prepares us to care for the outward woman in a harmonious way.

Beauty is inside out.

Outside in is backwards, pretentious, for it isn't beauty at all.

It is vanity which is preoccupation with beauty.

Vanity is easily recognizable.

People run from it.

Knowing we belong to God makes us feel beautiful perhaps for the first time.

This is true beauty's launch.

How then do we live out God's truths in such a way that the outward woman reflects a practical God honoring approach to beauty which makes the loveliness of virtue apparent?

This is basic inner beauty 101.

Our God is a God of excellence.

Excellence means being the best we can be.

Taking care of our bodies involve nutrition and hygiene.

Our skin, hair and teeth require systematic care.

There is no substitute for sleep.

Make up won't conceal the ravage of fatigue.

Make up is temporary.

Make up should enhance not scream for attention.

There are people trained to objectively to help women in this arena.

If you need help, find someone.

Wrinkles come.

Skin is hereditary.

Premature aging of the skin comes from our gene pool and sometimes from a difficult life.

Good habits can make a difference.

My mother Frances died at age 82 but her skin looked 50.

She avoided the sun and even in old age the practical beauty habits of her life produced the aura of winsomeness found in a lady.

Not everyone is so fortunate.

God's beauty is an inside job and sometimes the outside is a mirror as well.

We honor God by personal care of our bodies.

When we do not care at all we let God down.

Beauty is behavior.

It should be learned, caught and taught by a Godly mother or guardian not modeled from movie or fashion gurus. There is a great deficiency here in families. When godly mothers are in absentia, modesty is not pre eminent and therefore not learned as an element of God's beauty in dress, behavior and style. Modesty does not call attention to itself. It is restrained loveliness.

If you have never had anyone present this element of beauty, ask God for one in prayer. He knows what is missing and can bring women into your life to mentor you who possess His beauty inwardly and outwardly.

Restraint is a beautiful component to balance for it understates.

Excess smothers and overstates.

Our God is a God of balance and order.

…I am present with you in spirit and delight to see how orderly you are and how firm your faith in Christ is.[14]

We should endeavor to make our bodies strong.

When we are overweight we are out of balance.

When we are emaciated, we are weak and out of balance.

Weight involves balance.

She girds her loins with strength.[15]

The world He created has balance and order. We substitute food for the current vacuum in our lives…comfort, rejection, intimacy. We withhold food for the same reasons.

Every home should have a full length mirror.

Why?

A head to toe perspective will reveal what is and what is not.

Every day we must look at our bodies from all angles, front and back. We should do this in clothing stores before we bring home something that does not fit.

While we are looking at our bodies to see what is there we can look at the clothes we have chosen.

If something is too snug, too revealing, too short, too long, too plain, too frivolous, too uncomfortable, too outrageous, it will be apparent.

There will be no balance.

If the shoes or accessories dominate, we are minimized. Color and proportion are important. Know your body shape. Maximize your strengths and dress the flaws with care. Collars frame. Ruffles soften. Large prints overwhelm. Small prints refine. Bulky fabrics add bulk. Silky fabrics cling. Solid neutrals are a background for prints and color like a canvas. They create illusion. Jackets crop or elongate the body. Skirts are about choosing the most flattering length for your leg. Jewelry gently or boldly accentuates the face. Shawls and scarves layer a fitted look with color. When you look in the mirror what do you see? Do you see yourself or what you are wearing?

Excess is our culture.

God wants to teach restraint.

Less is always better.

God's beauty is not about style for style is developed through trial and error.

Godly character has guidelines to help affect the choices we make.

Too sensual, too revealing speaks graphically about you and detracts from the God you know.

What are you saying by how you dress?

Life with God should be a beauty watch.

Nature speaks of His beauty. Look out your window.

Art reveals His beauty. Integrate and enjoy it.

Express His beauty through living and bearing His image. Choose wisely.

Nobel Peace prize winner, Gabriella Mistral affirms God's beauty for she says, "Beauty…is the shadow of God over the universe."

His shadow is a shelter.

Come to the Shelter.

His beauty remains.

Keep watch over beauty.

His beauty strengthens.

A WATCHFUL EYE

1. Where have I learned my concept of beauty?
2. Can God speak to me through art?
3. Am I characterized by excess or restraint in my life?
4. What adjustments do I need to make?

WATCHWORD
The pain passes. The beauty remains.

— Renoir

PRAYER WATCH

Beautiful Lord;

Who speaks to us as a summer rain falls softly against our window and who invites us to the dawn's pastel light,

We bow down in awe of the beauty in this world which YOU have created and given to us to embrace.

Everywhere we look YOUR Imprint is there.

The heavens declare YOUR Glory.

The cloud cover protects and the sky frames the sun and the moon.

The earth responds to the seasons by pruning and blooming, blowing and snowing, raining and gaining harvest.

Nature births surprises.

A discovery of three blue eggs in a nest in one of my bushes was an artistic delight.

Beauty abounds as life waits.

The ocean's daily ebb and flow mark time and roar the promise of replenishing renewal.

We hunger for YOUR BEAUTY.

The artist forces us to face our own frailties.

YOUR WORD shows how to come home again.

The choices we make to reflect YOUR BEAUTY will require more than cosmetic surgery.

Open our hearts, Lord and reveal to us what needs to go.

Remove rebellion.

Restore the broken places.

Reinstate our God cognizance so we can see YOU in all things.

Give us a yearning to reflect YOUR BEAUTY in our lives so that the words we speak, the places we go, the clothing we wear, the behavior we bear, the investments we choose will be balanced in godliness.

Thank YOU for guiding us.

YOUR BEAUTY STRENGTHENS.

We will keep watch over beauty.

In Jesus' Love we receive and recover what was lost for now it is found.

My heart overflows in gratitude.

CHAPTER FOUR

HEALTH WATCH

If I can stop one heart from breaking, I shall not live in vain.
— Emily Dickinson

Health needs a watch.

Sleep, nutrition and exercise are integral for good physical health.

Our bodies have rhythms to establish for well being. They operate at optimum mode when we have established good habits of care.

We understand that body composition includes blood, water, bone and tissue mass. An average adult body carries 5-6 liters of blood and is two thirds water. It is made up of molecules, cells and organ systems which have intricate functions. The average body contains 206 bones. Our blood is critical to health. "It provides important nourishment to all body organs and tissues and carries away waste materials. Sometimes referred to as 'the river of life,' blood pumps from the heart through a network of blood vessels called the circulatory system. It regulates the body. In running a marathon, blood volume decreases but in pregnancy it increases." [1] It operates like fuel in a mighty engine as it passes through the organs of the body carrying oxygen and eliminating toxins while stabilizing body temperature along the way. There is power in the blood. It is strength to the body, the river of life.

Bodies need sleep.

The average body needs between 7-9 hours a day. "When human bodies do not get enough sleep, they tend to lose strength, the immune system decreases, and there is an increase in blood pressure. It can affect concentration, memory, logical reasoning and ability to do math."[2] Sleep is not an option for good health.

Bodies need nutrition.

In our society food is a preoccupation. We now have research we can read defining for us what we should eat so we can become accountable for our choices. There are food groups that our bodies need every day. According to *The My Pyramid Five Food Groups* guide, which is color- coordinated, we also get a special instruction to go along with the food group. Orange is grains "make half your grains whole," green is vegetables "Vary your veggies," red is fruits "focus on fruits," blue is milk "get your calcium rich foods," purple is meat "go lean with protein."[3] Proper food creates energy which strengthens us for work and play.

Bodies need exercise.

We run from this reality. Trainer, author, coach Tom Venuto says, "What happened to the idea of exercising every day because it's a positive habit that is good for you?" In other words where is common sense? Daily exercise that fits your stage, age and body is not popular any more. Instead we have designer marketing programs that promise to change our bodies in one 11 minute session or revolutionize us with one 30 minute program a week. Then we are also told that we can eat and indulge on some plans, with the promise of losing weight without exercise. Time out! This is deception! If musicians practiced this regimen there would be no music. If singers attempted to sing once in awhile, imagine what they would sound like.

Our bodies are begging for DAILY exercise.

Daily means daily.

Our bodies are wearing out for lack of exercise.

"What I am talking about is doing some form of moderate exercise – enough to break a sweat, bringing your heart rate up almost every day of the week. Why every day? Because that makes a habit and you develop a metabolic momentum." [4] In Dr. Michael Colgan's book, *The New Nutrition*, he tells us, "In order to keep the metabolic rate churning, frequent exercise is the key." He then concludes that 30 minute work outs 5 days a week is so much better for the body than 70 minute work outs 3 times a week. The message is this: find a way to move your body daily. When you do it is strengthened.

We have lots of resources to help us keep watch over our bodies. We need help.

Dr. Michael Debakey, pioneer heart surgeon lived until the age of 99 years. At age 96 he was still writing articles for medical magazines. His daily routine was to rise at 5 am and write for two hours. Then he drove to the hospital at 7:30 am and worked until 6 pm. He ate lightly during the day and enjoyed a main dinner meal with his wife. After dinner he retired to read and write for a couple of hours before bedtime. He walked everywhere he could as much as possible. He was described as a slender man who could fit into his military uniform even as he aged. His personal habits did not include smoking or alcohol. He lived a healthy lifestyle and had a remarkable mind that served him well as long as he lived. News writers Todd Ackerman and Eric Berger of The Houston Chronicle wrote a tribute to Dr. Debakey in 2008. In it they quoted his own words as he glimpsed a living heart for the first time. Dr. Debakey said, "I saw it beating and it was beautiful, a work of art. I still have an almost religious sense when I work on the heart. It is something God makes and yet we have to duplicate it."

Our bodies need a plan for health.

Our spiritual lives do also.

As a man thinks in his heart, so is he.[5]

Spiritual lives need a health watch on the heart.

Search me O God and know my heart; test me and know my thoughts; See if there is any offensive way in me and lead me in the way everlasting.[6]

Our hearts are at the core of our spiritual being and they must be kept fit.

When we ask God to search our heart, we are asking him to reveal to us what is offensive.

Our sin offends.

Confession to God cleans up our messes and prepares our hearts for His goodness.

Knowing your weaknesses and naming them brings strength for it is a heart of integrity that God desires.

He purified their hearts through faith.[7]

When we neglect this spiritual practice, we become dull, listless, frail and finally weakened in our faith.

Sin weakens.

If we do not own this spiritual discipline by habit we can be deceived by our hearts.

Man looks at the outward appearance but God looks at the heart.[8]

The heart is deceitful above all else and desperately wicked.[9]

A heart that operates outside of God's guidance will fall into decadence.

A healthy intimacy with God is a barometer for a spiritual heart.

Why?

A praying life yearns to be in His presence in order to grow in fellowship with Him.

He loves to be loved and "He is the supply for more love."[10]

Pour out your heart to him.[11]

That's what praying brings.

A purposeful life lives in His Word which instructs us daily and pumps vitality into our spiritual hearts.

I will put my laws in their hearts.[12]

Fix these words of mine in your heart.[13]

That's life in the Word.

What happens when we neglect our spiritual hearts?

They get blocked and cease to function in the full potential of His love or develop leakage losing Godly enthusiasm for living. Both blockage and leakage decimate energy. We become weak and apathetic, focusing on ourselves or hardened and critical, focusing on the imperfections of others.

Freed from this by daily confession of sin, we learn to love the presence of God. He then creates within us the shelter we must have in order to live vibrantly.

Prayer is a shelter anywhere we are for it is established in the human heart by a steadfast surrender to a Savior who sustains us.

A spiritual heart is maintained through a conscious feeding in God's Word and the exercise of prayer penetrating all the vital aspects of life. This balance brings strength when disaster strikes. Finding God's strength releases peace, boldness and a bedrock continuity in the One who holds life together.

At this point, faith surges. It is visible and the world watches.

When a genuine health crisis comes to the physical body, faith in God moves the spiritual heart to beat and live as a champion.

Standeth God in the shadow keeping watch over his own.

— James Russell Lowell

American television commentator and anchor Tony Snow, who became a White House Press Secretary, began his career in the media in 1979 as an editorial writer for the Greensboro Record in North Carolina. He graduated from Davidson College in 1977 with a degree in philosophy. His parents instilled in him common sense values such as hard work and serving others, for his dad was a teacher and his mom a nurse. His writing career led him to editorial positions with The Newport News, Virginia Daily Press, Detroit News and Washington Times. Eventually he became a syndicated columnist and America became aware of his talent. Mr. Snow was known to be gregarious and affable with many interests. Musically he played 5 instruments: saxophone, trombone, piccolo, accordion and guitar and he also played in a DC cover band called *Beats Workin'*. Known as an avid movie buff he was a sports enthusiast as well who made time for his Cincinnati Reds. Diagnosed with colon cancer in 2005, he died in 2008 at the age of 53, leaving behind his wife Jill and three children, Robbie, Kendall and Kristi. People from around the world offered moving tributes to this man. Among them was the song, *We all Die Soldiers*, written by Vivian George and made into a musical video tribute. It was a photo montage that mirrored his zest for life and love for people. One can see visually that as colon cancer entered his life, the lively, handsome, ebullient face remained even though the disease began to strip away his future. His friendships flowed as his life did with boundless enthusiasm and fun. Correspondent Adam Housley remarked, "We should all have his energy, love of country and warmth."

In a Commencement address given at Catholic University in 2007 he spoke with pragmatic insight, "It's trendy to reject religious reflection as a grave offense against decency. That's not only cowardly. That's false. Faith and reason are knitted together in the human soul. So don't leave home without either one. When it comes to faith, I've taken my own journey. You will have to take your own. Here's what I know. Faith is as natural as the air I breathe. Religion is not an opiate, just the opposite. It is the introduction to the ultimate extreme sport. There is nothing you can imagine that God cannot trump. As Paul said, 'Faith is the substance of things hoped for, the evidence of things not seen.' Once you realize there is something greater than you out there, then you have to decide, 'Do I acknowledge it, do I act upon it? You have to at some point surrender yourself'."[14]

In an article for *Christianity Today* 2007 entitled *Unexpected Blessings of Cancer* he writes, "I don't know why I have cancer.... It is what it is – a plain and indisputable fact. Yet even while staring into a mirror darkly, great and stunning truths begin to take shape. Our maladies define a central feature of our existence: We are fallen. We are imperfect. Our bodies give out...God offers...grace. We don't know how the narrative of our lives will end but we get to choose how to use the interval between now and the moment we meet our Creator face to face.... We can fight with might...and faith to live fully, richly, exuberantly no matter how the days are numbered. We can open our eyes and hearts....We want lives of simple predictable ease – smooth, even trails as far as the eye can see, but God likes to go off road. He places us in predicaments that seem to defy our endurance and comprehension – and yet don't. The challenges that make our hearts leap and stomachs churn invariably strengthen our faith and grant measures of wisdom and joy we could not experience otherwise....Your quandary has drawn you closer to God, closer to those you love, closer to the issues that matter.... When you enter the valley of the shadow of death, things change.... Christianity is not something doughy, passive and soft.... The life of belief teems with thrills, boldness, danger, shocks, reversals, triumphs, and epiphanies....There is nothing wilder than a life of humble virtue – for it is through selflessness and service that God wrings from our bodies the most we could ever give, the most we could ever offer, the most we could ever do. Through such trials God bids us to choose: Do we believe or do we not? Will we be bold enough to love, daring enough to serve, humble enough to submit, and strong enough to acknowledge our limitations? Every day we lie in the same, safe and impregnable place – in the hollow of God's hand." [15]

Tony Snow found the Shelter.

In it he found how to live and take his watch.

We watched him.

His story strengthens us in our watch.

This incredible man of faith courageously lived his life with an inspired abandonment made possible by a God he served with deep love and assurance.

The spiritual heart he had carried him, for his hope was found in the promises of God and undergirded by prevailing prayer. He acted upon and surrendered to the moments given to him with joy and thanksgiving. He found the moment to be rich rewards.

What a heart!

Faith is the force of life.

— Leo Tolstoy

Adversity came but faith reigned.

"When going through adversity, watch out for pessimists, blamers and toxic personalities. Beware of people who try to talk you out of your dreams and goals. Spend time with optimists and encouragers. Seek out people of faith." [16]

A persevering heart of faith receives a crown.

Blessed is the man who perseveres under trial, because when he has stood the test, he will receive the crown of life that God has promised those who love him.[17]

Eternal life with God is life rewarded.

Our faith is stretched by stories of heroism which hold responsibility in one hand and resiliency in the other.

On January 16, 2009, US Airways flight 1549 carrying 155 passengers landed safely in the Hudson River in New York City – on purpose. Both engines had been subjected to foreign object damage, known as (FOD), by a double bird strike of geese. It was an emergency landing in which pilot Captain Chelsey Sullenberger made his decision based on skilled instinct honed by years of safety training and professional experience.

Dr. Ken Alabi, a PhD in mechanical engineering from Stony Brook University who works on multi-disciplinary software for aircraft and aerospace systems, penned an article to clarify the technical expertise displayed in such a landing. Dr. Alabi is also a member of The American Institute of Aeronautics and Astronautics. He writes, "There is no record to my knowledge, in the database of aviation accidents in which a commercial jet of that size and capacity has been set down on water that successfully (the engines did indeed break off). Large aircraft usually break apart on water impact or torpedo in as one piece (actually most pilots try to achieve the break up as this increases survivability)....What happens when an aircraft already in flight loses the power to generate speed necessary to maintain the lift (the pilot's nightmare)? What Captain Sullenberger did is unprecedented. He did not have a lot of altitude to maneuver a powerless aircraft. He apparently set the plane down at the perfect angle such that it did not break up or tunnel into the water (think how to skip a flat stone on still water – it had to be thrown…at the right angle to glance off the surface). It takes an individual who is an extremely skilled pilot on multiple aircraft types, and is so attuned to his aircraft to accomplish that (and even then possibly some additional good fortune – right surface pressure and conditions, little tide or roughness, good weather, and low winds to list a few). Not surprisingly, this individual who has been flying since the age of 14 was a former Air Force pilot, and an aircraft safety consultant. His actions are a reflection of the American Spirit that never gives up and stares down adversity with a can-do attitude." [18]

The phenomenal feat of landing a plane in a river without any loss of life was truly a "Miracle on the Hudson." The graphic photograph of the cockpit of the plane bellied down in the placid but chilly winter water with its tail rising in the back and wings flanked with people standing waiting to be rescued will forever grip American hearts with amazing grace. It might be characterized creatively as a mammoth silver whale nesting in calm seas keeping watch over her precious young. Passengers describe the moments before landing. The pilot said, "Brace for impact because we are going down." Paul Jorgenson turned to the passenger seated next to him and asked the question, "Are we going to die?" His seat mate silently shook his head without speaking, nodding a yes…. Vallie Collins texted her husband, "my plane is crashing." Dave Sanders described the atmosphere in the cabin as "controlled chaos." As water started pouring in, male passengers shouted, "women and children first!" 19

Andrew Gray looked at this fiancé who was crying, took her by the hand and kissed her and said, "I love you," and started praying. People aboard were praying as they started their descent into the Hudson River. The frantic prayers turned into thankful jubilation. "God was certainly looking out for all of us," remarked Andrew Jamison. Fred Beretta concurred, "A lot of people just started praying and collecting themselves."

Robert Bea, a civil engineer who cofounded UC Berkeley's Center for Catastrophic Risk Management said, "When a plane is getting ready to crash with a lot of people who trust you…it is a test. Sully proved the end of the road for that test. He had studied it, he had rehearsed it, and he had taken it to heart." 20

The quiet, humble self-effacing Captain had been trained to execute.

The passengers were carrying him in prayer.

The Lord of Life was keeping watch.

These survivors were given a second chance.

What did we learn from this miracle?

We were invited to internalize the celebration of an unlikely happy ending, to hear the passengers voice their fears and cry out to God in desperation, to comprehend the charity of community found in common ground when you are in crisis together, to take the next step whatever it may be, to view life as a gift, to have a chance to begin again.

Selflessness in danger causes faith to soar.

Belief and disbelief are side by side in audiences, at the market, in schools and on planes.

We learn from one another.

Keeping watch over health requires God cognizance, spiritual perception.

Our physical and spiritual lives are knitted together.

Just as the blood flows through our hearts and into our bodies to bring us life, our faith is strengthened by loving God through prayer. It regenerates a sluggish faith.

I pray that the God of our Lord Jesus Christ, the Father of glory, may give you a spirit of wisdom and revelation as you come to know him, so that, with the eyes of your heart enlightened, you may know what is the hope to which he has called you. [21]

Spiritual heart health is fed by meditating and digesting the Word of God.

When we make time to reflect and consider His words, we find ourselves "floating on the depths of God, held safely in the waters of his loving presence. This is a moment when 'deep calls to deep.' (Psalm 42:7) Like the joyful awareness of a loved one whispering softly in our ears we become aware of the intimately personal voice of God. We cannot pinpoint where it is coming from because suddenly it is within us, sounding with heightened clarity and immediacy, reverberating in the chambers of our heart. We know without a doubt who is speaking to us. Jesus is the good Shepherd, and his sheep know his voice." [22]

When we learn to linger in the Word and contemplate it, it becomes food for our spiritual bodies and then transforms our hearts with strength.

To watch is to guard.

Our hearts need revitalizing daily as do our bodies.

Eat, rest, exercise, pray, study…some every day.

Encounter God.

As the infamous American humorist Erma Bombeck said long ago, "When I stand before God at the end of my life I would hope that I would not have a single bit of talent left and could say, 'I used everything YOU gave me'."

If we do we will have rescued a breaking heart.

To keep watch over health, our hearts must be kept fit and filled with faith, using all we have for His Glory.

We can.

Come to the Shelter.

Find His strength.

Keep watch.

A WATCHFUL EYE

1. Which area of the body do you neglect?
2. Is prayer a postscript or a principle in your life?
3. Have you asked God to give you a Hunger for His Word?

WATCHWORD
Some desire is necessary to keep life in motion.

— Samuel Johnson

PRAYER WATCH
Ever Present Father;
I am humbled at the work of faith in lives that seek YOU.

YOU must become more and I must become less.

I have followed after fads not faith.

I have lived extremes because I could.

I have neglected the life of my heart.

Prayer was a whim, at best a last ditch effort when all else failed.

The Bible was an outdated book, not a resource for living which I desperately need.

Forgive me.

Prone to wander Lord I feel it.

No wonder I have no victories.

I have lived in the shadows of false expectation.

I understand now that I was meant to live in the Word, to practice life in YOUR presence.

Draw me, Lord.

Remove the crust of self-reliance which has encased my heart.

I want to feel the pulse of YOUR LOVE.

Teach me to look and listen with eyes to see and ears to hear YOUR longing for me.

Move me daily to keep my watch.

Make me more than I am.

Mark my life with a passionate beating heart made ready to pour out YOUR Love to others.

Choose my way.

I choose YOU.

CHAPTER FIVE

LEGACY WATCH

Faith is a passionate intuition.

—William Wordsworth

A family watch requires vigilant strength.

One generation will commend your works to another. They will tell of your mighty acts. [1]

We are born into a heritage but we leave a legacy behind.

Your attic may reveal some clues to your heritage.

Mine did.

Prowling around one day in my parents' attic I found a box so utterly duct-taped (compliments of my father who was the duct-tape king) that I almost gave up my treasure hunt. Breaking a sweat I finally uncovered an outrageously over-sized maroon satin lamp shade from the 1940's that looked like an overdone hat. It was pleated and edged in a ruffled floral trim. Even though it possessed some fading, it dominated any room where it was placed and consequently over powered the original porcelain lamp that was in another duct-taped box, compliments of Dad. Wherever it was, you couldn't ignore it for there was no place it did not shout for attention. Weeks later I replaced it with a subtle substitute of ivory silk and Grandmother Isabella's lamp found a home in mine. Obviously she had passion for antiques and strangely enough I could not bring myself to get rid of the flamboyant lampshade. So I packed it up, stored it and labeled it for posterity. Who knows…it may have another life. I may wear it as a hat to a costume party. Mama Bella, my childhood name for my paternal grandmother, had lived in a simple farm house in the rural town of Burnsville, Mississippi, but apparently she had a longing for the lavish and ornate. Perhaps this lamp and its ostentatious shade lifted her life on the farm with joy every time she saw it. I believe it must have because someone else could not part with it. I was to be the recipient of a Pandora's Box from the past which provided a special look into my grandmother. Her heart must have yearned for beauty, which is a yearning for God. When she buried a fourteen year old son named Billy who died tragically from a careless kid's play with guns, his untimely death created a void she tried to fill up with beautiful things. Finally she found the Savior, who created His beauty within and gave her a comfort which carried her through the rest of her life. She penned her journey in essays confirming her faith and left it behind for me to read. They were in a box also.

My eccentric father, Cecil, loved his 1970's polyester one-piece jump suits all the way through the nineties. He would not part with any of the clothes he had saved through the years. When my parents' home was sold, it was time for a family rummage sale, encompassing 32 years of living in the last home they knew.

It threw him into a tailspin. "After all," he said, "these clothes are still good" even though he had not worn any of them for years. Can you imagine a pair of burgundy patent leather men's shoes? I can, for I sold them for $5.00. He was furious with me but logic prevailed because I was in charge. Secretly I boxed up two jumpsuits and gave them to his grandsons, Bren and Carey. One was a nondescript faded navy and the other was a putrid shade of mustard, both replete with expansion belts. One Christmas Eve years later at a family gathering Bren and Carey popped out before the gifts were opened, wearing them. We began to laugh hysterically. Dad was thoroughly delighted and said, "Mighty fine boys, those jumpsuits are still mighty fine." I found the navy one this week stashed in an attic box and remembered that my dear Dad wanted to keep everything. It was hard for him to let go of anything but in time God revealed to him that he could by allowing me to help him get there. His own father's anger and callousness had left my father bound by the past, unable to let go. The harsh words spoken to him as a young man in a family crisis were tapes that played over and over in his head for years. One day Dad and I came together in prayer and gave these tormenting words from the past to Jesus. They never played again. He forgave his deceased father. Release came from the past. In my Dad's final days of brain cancer, he sat up abruptly one morning in a time of confusion and suddenly spoke, "I have been to the top of the mountain and I know what's on the other side. That's where I am going." 2 God had given him a window of assurance, a glimpse of heaven. When he passed away there was the peace that passes understanding promised to the saints who let go of the world and hold on to Jesus. It is a task we must learn when we die but a reality we must live with in order to live.

The attic is a comfortable place for old things but we somehow seem to discover new things about ourselves as we look at what we collect. Grandchildren need some markers left behind which define our journey. After pondering many things in my heart one day I decided to box up and label some memories for the generations that follow me. There were objects that shaped our experience as a family. Our son Carey's Citadel Military College years, 1989-1992, with trophies, plaques and uniforms, have found a temporary home in a box. Our daughter Kellye's year as Miss America, 1987 presented us with loads of framed memorabilia, scrapbooks, costume jewelry and an adorable evening hat – all waiting for a season of unveiling. My husband Roy's years in the Navy, 1963-1993, are in boxes overflowing with plaques, framed photos, flight gear, uniforms and jackets. These mementoes represent life as we knew it to be.

Know the condition of your flocks. Pay careful attention to your herds.[3]

In all the years of my Navy life, I prayed, "Teach me how to live, Lord."

I began to think seriously about this process of legacy. What could I leave behind that might reveal our story and bring joy to our children, grandchildren and great grandchildren? Surely there would have to be some hints of wonderful moments of celebration that we shared. How could I put this together? One day I found myself wandering around an antique mall eyeing an old Lane cedar chest dated 1943. It was done in a warm oak color but was accentuated by some striped burling in a darker tone so it would fit anywhere. Yes, I decided I would begin gathering some favorite things, reflecting our heritage as a Navy family and also my parents' life. At present, I have placed four pairs of shoes into my chest. When mother had her first successful year in real estate she bought a pair of gray lizard sling back pumps accented in pale blue with a matching hand bag. Since the shoes are a size 9½, with a 6AA heel, no one will probably ever wear them...but I have them. She loved those shoes. As a child she never had shoes that fit so this was a purchase symbolic of status and childhood depravity. Dad loved his favorite brown loafers, keeping them polished and ready to wear but was most proud of his hats copied after the historic Alabama football coach Bear Bryant. One is a sporty tartan plaid of primary colors and one is a classy blonde beaver. Indeed he was spiffy in them. My grandmother, Mama Ofe, had a favorite pair of shoes that she wore to Kellye's wedding. Hers were vanilla cream leather with small silver heels. She said she "felt like a queen" in them. They are in my chest along with the shoes I wore to Kellye's wedding, being distinguished as the most expensive and the most comfortable shoes I ever had... period. My sister Judy and I argued about my shoes. She told me to buy expensive. I wanted to buy cheap because my dress was an evening gown which touched the floor. She told me I needed the best in order to weather the long evening. I caved in and purchased a pair made of burnished gold leather joined by a shapely feminine Machiavellian heel. Indeed I was able to stand and speak with 600 people that night for several hours without aching feet. The cost was a shameful $150.00 in 1989 which was so over the top that I budgeted for them and told no one until this moment. Now you have heard the rest of the story.

Feet are important for they affect how you walk.

In Cinderella's life one shoe made the difference.

A pair of comfortable well-made shoes will carry you through.

These pairs of shoes represent the heritage of a walking faith.

My godly heritage did walk by faith.

For we walk by faith not by sight. [4]

Mother lived through a tornado in Tupelo, Mississippi during which their home was destroyed.

Dad lived through a bankruptcy caused by an employee who stole money.

Mama Ofe had a son who was murdered and she forgave the murderer.

Mama Bella found her way home to heaven through a devastating grief.

When we walk in the light as he is in the light we have fellowship one with another. [5]

Our walk with the Lord involves choosing His path.

When I retired my golden shoes to the hope chest, it was with affection and memory. My sister Judy was right.

Inside there are also tee shirts from the Citadel football years, tee shirts from Kellye's Miss Tennessee and Miss America year along with Roy's U.S. Naval officer's hat and Carey's Citadel hat.

A lovely cream-white peignoir set embellished with pink rosettes, which was for my wedding trousseau, is alongside our wedding album as well as a few bundles of blue ribbon-bound letters that Roy and I wrote to each other in our year of courtship. Those love letters are the only ones I saved. They unfold our romance and our heart's desire to be husband and wife forever. At this moment this is the assortment my treasure chest holds but there is room waiting for future treasures. I have other collections in special decorative containers. My antique chest now resides in our keeping room as a reminder of our beginnings. Family pictures rest on top and Norman Rockwell prints with beagles hang on the wall framing this nostalgic piece which holds the story of a family – ours.

The past is never dead. It's not even past.

— William Faulkner

Heritage is a place from which the shelter of legacy is built.

Ring Lardner cites in the book *The Heritage*, "The family you come from isn't as important as the family you're going to have."

So we are privileged to keep watch day by day over the legacy we will leave behind through choice, will, commitment and faith.

What will our watch be?

Where will it take us?

Whom will it involve?

Once in awhile a startling account of keeping watch over legacy surfaces.

Such was the story of Polish social worker Irena Sendler who served in the Polish underground and Zergota resistance organization during World War II in German-occupied Warsaw. Her position as an employee of the Social Welfare department gave her special permit to enter the Warsaw Ghetto and check for typhus. "She organized the smuggling of Jewish children out of the Ghetto, carrying them out in boxes, suitcases and trolleys." [6] So great was her compassion for these children that "under the pretext of conducting inspections of sanitary conditions during a typhoid outbreak, Sendler visited the ghetto and smuggled out babies and small children in ambulances and trams, sometimes disguising them as packages. [7] The children were placed with Polish families or convents. She kept their real names in a jar to keep track of their original identities. The organization Zergota assured the children that when the war was over, they would be returned to their Jewish relatives. [8] She eventually was arrested by the Gestapo and brutally tortured but escaped by aid of the Zergota. Remaining in hiding until the end of war, Irena Sendler continued her work for the Jewish children. After the war, jars containing their true heritage buried in the ground were dug up and attempts were made to find their parents. Unfortunately most had been exterminated or were missing. At this time she was also imprisoned and persecuted by the Communist Polish state authorities. Mrs. Sendler was nominated for the Nobel Peace Prize. In her elderly years she was cared for in a nursing home until her death by Elzbieta Ficowska, one of the infants she saved. Posthumously Mrs. Sendler received the Audrey Hepburn Humanitarian Award in May 2009. It is an award given for helping children. Its citation recalls that "Irena

Sendler's heroic efforts saved two and a half thousand Jewish children during the occupation of Poland in World War II."[9]

More than 4000 pages of research have been compiled by college students on her life. She told students in 2002, "You cannot separate people based on their race or religion. You only separate people by good and evil. The good will always triumph."[10]

The fair countenance of this endearing Polish woman is a picture of deep satisfaction. A merry quality peeks out of determined eyes that twinkle with vision; a cherub in disguise on mission was she.

In a letter to the Polish Parliament she says, "Every child saved with my help is the justification of my existence on this earth, and not a title to glory."[11]

A Polish woman kept watch over the legacy of Jewish children.

Her physician father, whose life of giving impacted hers, died of typhus himself. Later on Irena said, "I was taught that if you see a person drowning you must jump into the water to save them whether you can swim or not."[12]

She did.

This was her heritage.

Her legacy included leaving behind a generation of Jewish children to live and uncover theirs.

Her watch was enlarged to include many who were not of her personal lineage and so may ours.

Life in a jar became life preserved.

We live out what we know.

We leave behind our investments.

We are accountable to God for what we have been given.

In Psalm 127, we are given a picture of God's plan for the family.

Unless the Lord builds the house, the builder labors in vain.

Unless the Lord watches over the city, the watchmen stand guard in vain.

Sons are a heritage from the Lord, children a reward from him. Like arrows in the hands of a warrior are the children of one's youth....

Life with God requires training.

If we build we become workmen.

If we guard we are watchmen.

If we pattern godliness for our children they become warriors.

Author Nancy Leigh DeMoss offers counsel, "The picture here is a battlefield – our sons and daughters are ammunition. They are arrows in the battle, and God intends we release and send them out into the culture.... The psalmist tells us there is a house to be built, a city to be guarded and a battle to be fought. If the workmen cut corners, if the watchmen fall asleep or get distracted while he's on his shift, or if the warrior fails to show up for battle...lives can be endangered. These are vital strategic roles.... God is building His Kingdom. Our children are a sacred stewardship from the Lord." [13]

A watch over legacy will involve your whole life.

Children are all different.

Each one has abilities and talents that must be identified and then affirmed constantly. Find the unique in each. Character involves living from a core of values. Have one. Time is a commodity that one never seems to have enough of but we all have the same amount – 24 hours a day. Use it well. Money runs out, not in; and so we have to understand its place and not allow it to reign as a god.

Sometimes we mess up as parents. Apologize.

Sometimes children mess up. Forgive.

Sometimes God sees a different outcome than we do. Trust.

Sometimes we almost give up. Don't.

Scripture says, *Train up a child in the way he should go.*[14]

Our children are a gift from the Lord.

Don't forget this on days you want to abdicate parenting.

We don't bring them into this world by ourselves.

They are His Plan.

When we submit our lives unto Him day by day, HE will lead us through the brief seasons of parenting for all too soon it ends.

Time comes, goes and so do they.

I knew I must seize the time I had and seek God about how to make it memorable.

Our nomadic military life as a family necessitated that home be categorized as what we took with us in a moving van and sorted once we found the house. It was always a decorator's challenge but I loved defining the rooms of the many homes in which we lived.

Roy's career involved Navy deployments, which were months spent away from home aboard a U.S. Navy ship. I had time to mull over the significance of daily living and I found I was drawn to pursue a Life with God.

These lengthy separations (thirteen and one-half years, cumulatively, in a thirty year career) kept us from sharing many special holidays together with Roy. It became my heart's desire to devise a way to include him as we planned.

Therefore I learned from my Navy wife watch of many years that I must value each day and learn to celebrate.

The clock was ticking in my children's lives.

Dad was missing out.

I was crying out in prayer for creative ways to cement celebration into the foundation of our home.

God answered.

When Kellye graduated from Poway High School, in Escondido, CA in 1983, her Dad would be at sea as the Air Wing Commander aboard the carrier USS Coral Sea. This was a world cruise. He left from San Diego, CA and would return stateside to the east coast in Norfolk, VA the following year. We would move there but there would be many obstacles to overcome before this was a reality.

Graduation Day was coming for Kellye.

I prayed, "Lord, help to make this day special for her. Show me how to include Roy. He must be a part of this celebration. Only YOU can show us how to do this."

He did.

I wrote her father and asked him to write something…a letter, a poem, and some thoughts that I might present to her from him. He wrote an amazing acrostic poem which spelled the letters of her name on the left and then ended with the letters of her name on the right.

It was filled with a father's love, affirmation, expectation and dreams for her future.

I wept when I received it for I kept thinking all daughters and sons should have such a gift.

I wondered how any child could let down such a father?

My charge was to have it done in calligraphy, framed for a college dorm and presented to her in a way she would not forget. After much thought I arranged to have a Graduation Tea and my mother and grandmother flew out for the occasion. It would be their gift to Kellye. She invited her friends and though many of them had never attended a Graduation Tea the idea was to gather your community of family and friends to share memories and have fellowship. My dear friend Pat Karlin baked a fantastic three-tiered, white cake embellished with white rosettes, and on top was a 'Precious Moments' figurine of a little girl with a diploma in hand. As Kellye entered the room, her father's poem was framed and positioned on an easel. It took her breath. Tears flowed. Joy came. His presence was there in his words.

Today this poetic milestone hangs in her kitchen.

In 1983 there was a critical gold shortage. I had prayed about a gift from me for Kellye. Earlier in the year, I realized she would only wear a class ring for that year so I suggested we look at a ring she might wear forever. We chose a small gold pinkie ring with pave diamonds and it was affordable. Yeah God! Then I pondered some more about the gold dilemma and decided I would collect all the gold charms I had been given for a bracelet I no longer wore and have them melted down and made into two different gold nugget loveliers, one for me and one for Kellye. In Kellye's nugget of gold, tiny diamonds from my

Mother's first wedding band were placed. Therefore her nugget contains her mother's gold and her Nana's diamonds.

Today she wears this ring beside her wedding band.

Legacy created in jewelry.

Gifts can be signposts.

When Carey graduated in 1988, Dad wrote a poem for him and I put together a scrapbook of photographs from boyhood to high school emphasizing the theme of athletics in his life. I gave him a watch engraved with scripture; The *joy of the Lord is my strength*. He is a Navy Chaplain today and his poem follows him around as he moves, each time finding a home on a wall. His children love the scrapbook of his youth.

I also wrote each of my children a letter when they graduated from high school – a release.

They did not need it.

I did.

When they married I wrote a letter releasing them again.

They did not need it.

I did.

I spent a lifetime mothering so God had to show me how to let go...in stages.

He did.

God will see to it that we mother others as well; friends, animals, sometimes strangers placed in our path.

Elie Wiesel reminds us, "Friendship marks a life even more deeply than love. Love risks degenerating into obsession. Friendship is never anything but sharing."

Our legacy must include mentoring one another for our sharing bonds us.

Rites of passage come and must be punctuated, celebrated.

After grandchildren came along and began to grow up, I began to think and pray about a way to mark their transition into the teen years. Author Patrick Morely wrote a book called *Young Man in the Mirror*. In it he discusses the rite of passage in a young man's life.

Our Jewish friends are way ahead of us. We all learn from one another. In their religious tradition, this process for a boy is called a Bar Mitzvah and for a girl, a Bat mitzvah.

We can borrow their model.

Brady would be the first grandson to turn 13.

A terrific idea began to form. Plan a rite of passage birthday at age 13 and invite about 12 special friends that a young man would choose. These would be men who had influenced him; grandfathers, uncle, cousins and friends like coaches, teachers and mentors. The father would moderate. Each man would write a life lesson. My job would be to prepare a personalized book in which these special affirmations could be inserted. They would share a meal together and each man would speak his lesson forging a bond of support. It would then it would be placed into the memory book. They would close in prayer over him and pledge to be a part of a lifelong circle of faith to him. His memory book would reflect his heritage.

We began this celebration birthday with Brady, followed, in order, by Caleb, Justice Luke and, in proper time, Nathanael.

Cassidy was the first granddaughter to turn 13 and in proper time Phoebe, Ella Joy and Bea will join her.

Since Cassidy's birthday was in December before Christmas, her other Grandmother Mimi held a Tea at her home. Kellye moderated and 12 women were chosen to come alongside and impart life lessons. I made the book. This was an intimate time of laughter, prayer and encouragement as godly women gathered to surround Cass with His love. Little did we know that Mimi would suddenly be taken ill with cancer in 2008, swiftly leaving us a few days after Mothers' Day. While we were visiting there the weekend before she died, I saw Cassidy's memory book opened on the kitchen counter to the page where Mimi had written her some precious common sense words of wisdom.

Written words are remembered.

Rites of passage, and celebrations which launch our youth into teenage life can fortify a shield of safety, a hedge of prayer, a strengthening from seasoned saints shored up for the trials ahead that will surely come.

We are workmen building homes.

We are watchmen who pray protection.

We are raising warriors to take their place in this world.

Our legacy can change this nation…again.

Graduation Day has now come for Brady Cash Sheppard, Kellye and Todd's son.

College is around the bend.

The third generation must be launched.

My husband is known as Poppy and I am known as Honey to our grandchildren.

Poppy has his poem written for Brady and I have it framed.

Honey has written a prayer of faith and expectation for Brady's future. We are ready to celebrate.

For the Lord watches over the way of the righteous.[15]

He is watching us as we take our watch over our families.

"God would want the latter years of our lives to be exceedingly fruitful – a time of influence and opportunity, years when we synthesize the wisdom gained from a lifetime of experience, years when we impart strength to emerging generations. In a way these years are a test of all we truly believe. The Lord wants us to succeed to the last. He wants us to finish strong."[16]

Fill up a hope chest with some practical symbols of your journey of faith.

Leave behind the signature of God upon your life.

Shoes, clothing, jewelry, photographs, favorite things…a jar or a book.

In Christ your legacy continues.

For the Lord is good and his love endures forever; his faithfulness continues through all generations.[17]

Come to the Shelter.

Find strength to keep watch.

A WATCHFUL EYE

1. What is it about your heritage that you find difficult to accept?

2. What can you do to leave behind a legacy of faith?

3. Can God teach you to mark your life with His celebration in spite of circumstance?

WATCHWORD
What you leave behind is not what is engraved in stone monuments, but what is woven into the lives of others.

— Pericles

PRAYER WATCH

Beloved Father of Generations;

How faithful YOU are.

We come and bow down in thanksgiving for the journey of parenting.

Strengths and weaknesses emerge.

We must honor virtue and build homes of moral character.

Sometimes it is pure joy.

Sometimes it is certain struggle.

When our children are born the heritage of both families is reproduced.

Babies awaken us to a life that can no longer be self centered.

As they progress through the stages of childhood and into young adult life we do also.

Parenting is a side by side experience.

Help us walk in faith, Lord.

Our watch is critical.

Faith in YOU is the prize that will carry them through.

It carried us.

In this journey our Christian family will enlarge to include brothers and sisters, sons and daughters YOU bring to us.

Thank YOU, Lord for in YOUR Strength we shall prevail.

TRIBUTE TO KELLYE

Kellye – Born of pure unbounded love;

 Heart and soul an angel

Entered a life full of joy…

 And made it bloom, as sea and sky

Looked on with soothing temper

 And restless spirit

Likened to the soft breeze, a wind of

 Every place, imagined, untouched

Yet stilled by wise direction, a guiding

 Hand sought, taken…held

Each smile reflected, each tear

   Consoled in gentleness, the silent tal**K**

   The strong touch and sense

   Of purpose given in presence and absenc**E**

   Wonderfully embraced and

   Fostered in every life experience unti**L**

   Very quickly, all too soon

   That innocent love, the child, my wil**L**

   And image through and through

   Becomes the fullness of God's intent and m**Y**

   Humble, yet proud bequest

   To a breathless world, my heart – Kelly**E**

Love, Dad

6-15-1983

TRIBUTE TO CAREY

Carey – the very name is legacy,

    in the respect and honor rendered in its giving,

Another refrain in the song of life,

    now made more melodic and fulfilling, ideal

Reflection of the gentle love

    which brought forth the man, the strength

Entwined through the moral lyric;

    the character boldly embodied in the spirit of

Youth, measured and matured into the man who,

                With wings spread, soaring to olympi**C**

                 heights, his goals set high and true,

             will reach the mark. As relentless as the se**A**

             will be the endeavor, till, transcending

            even purest vision, this son's destiny is clea**R**

    ...the world will note the passing of this man,

                for nothing of worth will be the sam**E**

       on this earth. A new era has, indeed, begun:

       The door's opened God's blessings on — Care**Y**

Dad

Graduation Day '88

Chapter Six

Liberty Watch

Eternal vigilance is the price of liberty.
— Thomas Jefferson

Liberty will require a watch of faith.

In the year 2008, I was drawn into a watch of intense prayer over my nation which was at once a weight of warning and a disturbing wonder which I could not fathom.

I felt consumed while at the same time carried by His Unlimited Resource.

I wept for almost a year.

This was not depression but focused expression given to release the ominous anxiety that was gathering in one hand and the positioning of a purposeful dependence upon the Living God in the other.

Both hands were opened to receive.

An oxymoron evolved for in my weakness I became strong.

My spiritual eyes were strangely keen to the subtle undercutting of liberty in our society. It was a movement disguised as an innovative push with promises of prosperity and provision for all.

The price tag was unknown then and is still ambiguous but the cost would be incomprehensible.

I wrestled with feelings of fear and angst as I searched God's Word for a direction that men and women of intentional faith could pursue.

I found it.

Jesus answered... *You must follow me.*[1]

So I looked back historically and began to see the unraveling of a nation whose walls were now crumbling from the lack of a moral compass.

Our founders came to America for religious liberty. They expressed it in varying ways. George Washington wrote a letter to John Armstrong in which he said, "I am sure there never were a people, who had more reason to acknowledge a Divine interposition in their affairs then those of the United States."[2] Benjamin Franklin stood up before the Constitutional convention and said, "The longer I live sir, the more convincing proofs I see of this truth, that God governs in the affairs of men."[3] "In review of 15,000 items from the founders...the Bible can be credited in some way for 94% of the quotes of the founding fathers."[4]

Therefore we can ascertain that the influence of the Bible was prevalent then and the people who wrote our founding documents, the Constitution and the Declaration of Independence, were people who reverenced God.

There are many historical references available for us to study and decipher the mindset of those who came here. Their diversity did not fracture the foundation they laid. Discovering who they were is a personal journey worthy of our investment.

The overriding truth I found was this: they came for liberty.

The trail of liberty is easily documented.

We have the stories of our wars and the many sacrifices made by leaders who laid down their lives as they served our nation.

In the *American Minute*, an article entitled "Four Chaplains" dated February 3, 1943 reveals the circumventing unity faith brings.

The story revolves around the Allied Ship Dorchester, which was plowing the waters near Greenland. Early in the morning a Nazi submarine torpedoed the ship and the explosion killed many on board. In this chaotic crisis, four chaplains; a priest, a rabbi and two protestant ministers worked as a team to distribute life jackets. When all the jackets were dispersed, the four chaplains took theirs off and placed them on four remaining young men. Standing together embracing a slanting deck, they bowed their heads in prayer as they sank to their icy deaths. Congress honored them by declaring this date as Four Chaplains Day. President Dwight Eisenhower remarked on February 7, 1954, "We remember that only a decade ago, aboard the transport, Dorchester, four chaplains of four faiths together willingly sacrificed their lives so that four others might live. In the three centuries that separate the Pilgrims of the Mayflower from the chaplains of the Dorchester, American's freedom, her courage, her strength, and her progress have had their foundation in faith. Today as then, there is need for positive acts of renewed recognition that faith is our surest strength, our greatest resource." [5]

This is liberty.

There is strength in liberty.

America has always had men and women who yielded themselves to the cause of liberty.

We are a land of free enterprise, inclusion, life, liberty and the pursuit of happiness.

A seemingly subtle shift in our character as a nation took place in the 1960's involving three court cases challenging our rights to expressions of faith such as the freedom to our pray in public schools.

The results still decimate our lives decades later.

In the case of Engel v. Vitale, 1962, a prayer was adopted by The New York education system to be spoken before the start of each day's classes. The prayer promoted good moral character, provided spiritual training and helped combat juvenile delinquency. It was non-sectarian and non denominational. It was so bland it was referred to as the "to whom it may concern prayer." Here it is: "Almighty God, we acknowledge our dependence upon thee, and we beg Thy blessings upon us, our parents, our teachers and our Country."[6]

What kind of prayer was it?

A simple prayer seeking God's blessing upon students, teachers, parents and our nation.

This opened the door for anti-God crusader Madelyn Murray O'Hair to file a law suit blocking prayer which ended up in the Supreme Court. How tragic that it was noted that not a single Christian organization filed a brief in support of school prayer.

Asleep on her watch of liberty, the church failed.

Simultaneously school prayer and Bible reading (Abington Township School District v. Schempp, 1963) were dealt the final blow with the Pennsylvania school system. Every day ten verses of scripture were read as the school day began without comment and with the caveat that if any student objected he could be excused. Sadly the High Court ruled that prayer and Bible reading were violations of the First Amendment.[7]

In sweeping judicial reform, finally, any overt call to God in school, any conscience concerning the reading of His Word was silenced.

Liberty stifled weakens a nation.

Would a prayer and the reading of the Word of God have interrupted the plans or erected a spiritual safeguard around Columbine High School in Littleton, CO in 1999 as two young men bent on destruction took out the lives of 12 students and a teacher before they ended their own lives?

We will never know.

Prayer is a shelter.

In 2001 a survey of High school students indicated that 17.4 % had carried a weapon to school during the 30 days preceding the survey.[8]

We are living in a time of increased school violence on secondary and college campuses involving irrational shootings, mindless murder, grave discontent and aggravated anger prodded by drug addiction.

We have a myriad of organizations formed to combat these risks like the National Criminal Justice Reference Service, National Institute on Drug Abuse, Teen Zeen, and faith based groups like Teen Challenge to aid teens in all of the above.

Our children need a godly standard to be raised once again in school.

We must return to a life that has a center in God Almighty. Our liberty as a nation is being reduced. If we do not reclaim righteousness, depravity will continue its downward spiral neutralizing faith and rendering a society of entitlement thinking rather than building up a God ordained dependence.

We were never meant to depend on government.

Liberty protects and strengthens the individual.

True Liberty is found through freedom in Christ Jesus.

Faith is a factor in freedom.

You will know the truth and the truth will set you free.[9]

Liberty and Justice go hand and hand.

Blessed are they who maintain justice, who constantly do what's right.[10]

We must seek to do what is right for our God who is a just God.

Disturbing statistics reveal the moral decline of our nation.

According to information released by the National Center of Health Statistics (NCHS) May 13, 2009, "America is rapidly becoming a nation of unwed parents. In 2007 1.7 million babies were born to unwed moms in their 20's and 30's. Four out of every ten babies are born to single moms. Today there is a de-emphasis on marriage and the family." [11]

The family is a powerful unit for stability in a nation.

When it is broken, our walls begin to crumble.

When we forget to provide for the weakest, our walls crumble.

Before I formed you in the womb I knew you.[12]

How awesome to read that our God knows about all of life even from conception; therefore, we are charged with protecting it.

When we forget the aged, our walls crumble.

Honor your father and mother.[13]

Caring for our parents, widows, orphans and others in society is mandated in scripture.

Seek justice, encourage the oppressed. Defend the cause of the fatherless, plead the case of the widow.[14]

When we forget the poor, our walls crumble.

There will always be poor in the land. Therefore I command you to be openhanded toward your brothers and toward the poor and needy in your land.[15]

The Word of God is a guide for living in society with awareness and integrity.

Faith in God is a foundation on which to build personal liberty in a nation.

Throughout history we have some who have zealously seized the quest for liberty at great cost.

Nobel Prize winner Alexandr Solzhenitsyn, the Soviet dissident author, was threatened by the KGB and thrown into prison in Moscow. His great work *The Gulag Archipelago* had been published in France. They threatened his family. He would not back down. His books were missiles of truth. Can one word of truth move the world? If so, then his words of truth have helped to liberate the spirit of man by deliberately reminding us what happens when a nation forgets God. He continues, "Patriotism means unqualified and unwavering love for the nation which implies not uncritical eagerness to serve, not support for unjust claims, but frank assessment of its vices and sins, and penitence for them."

Indeed his words ring out to us with the importance and the power of one.

Is faith still alive in America?

In an article entitled "The End of Christian America" written in *Newsweek* Magazine April 13, 2009, by Jon Meacham, he tackles the issue in many ways. Over the past two decades percentages of those who identified themselves as Christian have fallen, on page 36, he writes, "The Christian God isn't dead. But he is less of a force in U.S....culture than at any other time in recent memory."

Indeed it appears many have forgotten God.

According to Christian apologist Ravi Zacharias there have been three shifts in culture in the past 40 years which are significant.

First; "Secularization is the belief that religious ideas, institutions and interpretations have lost social significance. Beginning in the 1960s the moods of secularization led to the loss of shame." [16]

Morals and ethics do shape a society.

Secondly, he presents pluralization, which sounds like a good idea. However, in it there are many worldviews and no one is dominant. With it relativism enters and "if all moral choice is merely relative then there is no point of reference to right or wrong, hence the loss of reason." [17]

A core of belief is a center of ethics from which one operates.

Thirdly, privatization came as an accommodation to the religiously minded which was deemed okay as long as it was not brought into the public arena. "Those who believed in a spiritual Essence, an Ultimate Reality needed to keep those beliefs private, which led to a loss of meaning." [18]

Our language changed and so did our perception.

God is not dead in our land.

He is alive in the hearts of people who know Him but we have become derelict on our watch.

Believers must wake up and begin to live in the Word of God again.

God plus one is a majority.

One can change the world.

One did.

He made the way for us to do also.

His name is Jesus.

If we return to embrace a Christianity filled with fervor and boldness, fueled by a faith full of God's presence, forever empowered by the strength of God, we move the center of our lives, our homes, our community and our nation back to God.

Our leaders change.

Our God does not.

Blessed is the nation whose God is the Lord, the people He has chosen as His own inheritance.[19]

When we establish our hearts in service to our God we know liberty and we bring liberty to the home, marketplace, the school, the arts and even to the government.

We must not be silent.

We must take our place at the table.

We must engage our culture.

> *One starts an action simply because one must do something.*
> —T. S. Eliot

The world of movies brought to us a classic American drama birthed from the Novel *To Kill a Mockingbird* written by Harper Lee. It reveals the evolution of a nation writhing with bigotry and prejudice in the 1930's in Alabama. It is a story of the power of one, one man who took a stand for justice, who operated in a liberty born from character and lived out pragmatically in a sleepy southern town filled with elements of rage and hypocrisy. That man was Atticus Finch, a homegrown defense lawyer of principle and truth, a man who would not back down or quit. Traditional family values are seen in the Finch home. A widower father's responsibility is preeminent as he is intimately involved in all the decisions of the lives of his children. An African-American woman named Calpurnia is the "housekeeper nanny" to Scout and Jem. Their real names are Jean Louise and Jeremy. She provides the daily care in the home until bedtime and they respect and love her. She is a mother figure of character.

The characterizations are rich, with shades of southern innuendo. The narrative is spoken throughout the movie in the soothing reflective voice of actress Kim Stanley. She speaks as an adult recounting her years of growing up as Scout. It is moving and poignant as we listen for the brooding questions of childhood.

Today many of our children have been sabotaged from being children. The lack of good, solid parenting has pushed them into feeling they must look and act adult. They are stripped of the rightful progression of inquisitive innocence, the purity of the world of a child.

Harper Lee captures the gentility of custom and civility of this time with descriptions like this:

"Maycomb was a tired old town, even in 1932 when I first knew it. Somehow, it was hotter then. Men's stiff collars were wilted by nine in the morning. Ladies bathed before noon...and by nightfall were like soft tea cakes with frosting from sweating and sweet talcum. The day was twenty four hours long, but it seemed longer. There's no hurry for there is nowhere to go and nothing to buy...and no money to buy it with. Although Maycomb County had recently been told that it had nothing to fear but fear itself....That summer I was six years old." [20]

The preciousness of being a child, the moments of play and adventure that Scout and Jem had with their precocious summertime friend Dill, the treasure box filled with items given to them by Boo, the gentle, mentally handicapped neighbor who lived an isolated existence in the beginning of the drama, but later becomes a champion friend, are imprinted in their lives. The scenes at school, the meals at home, the normalcy and predictability of family life cast against the back drop of the Depression reveal family dynamics. This was a time in which poverty was real and folks possessed a conscious concern for life surrounding their neighbors. It was expressed with integrity and decency because a moral compass was in place.

I can identify with the transient children today who live with gaping holes of impermanence in their lives because my father's job caused us to move constantly and the 33 schools I attended left a yearning for life in a small town bred with familiarity. Even in spite of harsh circumstances, a child's imagination is alive.

It always is and we are made to grasp the scope of this story written from a child's perspective with poignant pause for we find ourselves in it somewhere.

The cruel contrast of racial violence is balanced by the moral courage of one man, Atticus Finch.

A simple, humble African-American named Tom Robinson is falsely accused of a criminal sexual act against an itinerant Caucasian young woman who was battered and abused by a demoralizing prejudiced father, a drunk.

The injustice is so blatant that it makes one shout for Truth to be gloriously acknowledged.

Atticus lives out the convictions of his life before his children.

He does not waver when fear and personal attacks come.

He continues to encourage Tom Robinson…to bring him hope against all odds.

The town gathers in the courthouse to listen, observe and come to conclusions.

The jury is given a final argument in which Atticus Finch unravels false morality and defines it from a basis of justice and truth, painting a true picture of shameful injustice based on the color of a man's skin, rather than on facts.

The closing remarks end with these words, "I am no idealist to believe firmly in our courts and of our jury system – that's no ideal to me. That is a living, working reality! I am confident you will review, without passion, the evidence you have heard, come to decision and restore this man to his family. In the Name of God, do your duty. In the Name of God, believe…Tom Robinson." [21]

This moment is a veil that parts and positions the opportunity for justice.

Atticus pleads for Tom in the Name of God but Tom ends up being convicted by a spineless, weak-willed jury.

Atticus loses the case but wins the moral imperative by raising up a standard.

Being a man who is known to be just, a man who is respected by all people in the community, we observe him in the last scene in the courtroom as he packs up and leaves dejectedly. The Reverend Sykes, an African-American preacher who has involved himself in this case by being present, diligently notices that Scout has fallen asleep and so he awakens her. The entire congregation of men and women with babies, old and young, has gathered there daily to keep watch over this spectacle. They hear the Reverend say, "Jean Louise, Jean Louise, stand up. Your father is passing by." [22]

Slowly but emphatically the entire body of people rises to their feet to pay homage to a man that selflessly fought for liberty and justice.

Succumbing to panic and fear the next day the accused Tom bolts running for his life and ends up losing it.

So much insight is woven into this powerful saga. The truths it presents are timeless and continue to resonate today. The title of the book and later movie comes from a discussion about when to use a gun and where to use it. Atticus explains to Jem that his father warned him that, "Sooner or later the temptation to go after birds would be too much and that he could shoot blue jays if he could hit 'em but it was a sin to kill a mockingbird because mockingbirds don't do anything but make music for us to enjoy. They don't eat people's garden, don't nest in the corncrib. They don't do one thing but just sing their hearts out for us." [23]

I could linger in this story forever and daily learn about liberty and justice.

Atticus Finch is the revelation of the power of one.

He embodies doing what is right.

His watch was one of liberty and justice.

So is ours.

One life matters.

The Lord watches over the way of the righteous but the way of the wicked will perish. [24]

Our God is calling us to keep watch over liberty.

In Psalm 106 we look at a rebellious people gone awry, one that blends in and secures its own agenda. The scripture reveals how they become diverted into pursuits of disobedience, distancing themselves from God.

Rebellion is not foreign.

The description is indicting and graphic.

They forget God but He does not forget them.

He is always watching.

They did not remember your kindnesses...and rebelled .... They soon forgot what he had done...they did not wait for his counsel. In the desert they gave into craving. In the wasteland they put God to the test. They grew envious of Moses and Aaron...and worshiped an idol cast from metal. They provoked the Lord to anger by their wicked deeds and a plague broke out. [25]

Willful sin brings judgment and consequence *BUT Phinehas stood up and intervened and the plague was checked. This was credited to him as righteousness for endless generations to come.* [26]

One conjunctive word – BUT – identifies the change that comes, for with it a man stands up and intervenes and the plague is stopped. He was remembered for generations for this act.

This man was following his God and when he needed to stand he was prepared.

The power of one embedded in real faith is enough to change the course of nations.

Why?

Righteousness and justice are the foundation of his throne. [27]

Our God reigns even when we feel helpless and everything looks hopeless.

A compromised life that caves into every whim caves a society.

Martin Luther King said, "Injustice anywhere is a threat to justice everywhere."

Therefore we must be alert and knowledgeable of history, government and the Word of God.

We must rediscover and reclaim our Life with God.

Preserving liberty is noble, critical, warranted and called for by the God we serve.

There is no wealth but Life.

— John Ruskin

God cognizance breeds a life conscious, committed and clarified through His Word.

We do not worship the Bible.

We worship the King of kings.

We are instructed in matters of living.

We serve from hearts desirous of pleasing Him, which means we must love what He loves.

He loves people.

He loves righteousness.

He loves liberty because He brought it to us through the Cross.

In partnering with Him, we are called to correct injustice.

In positioning His Word as our guide, we can live in assurance.

In petitioning Him for answers, we find a way through desperation and subjection…every time.

Words from Presidents raise the banner of liberty over us.

> *Liberty without learning is always in peril and learning without liberty is always in vain.*
>
> — John F. Kennedy
>
> *Freedom is never more than one generation away from extinction. We did not pass it on to our children in the bloodstream. We must fight for it, protect it and hand it over to them to do the same.*
>
> — Ronald Reagan

Come to the Shelter.

Live in God's Word.

Find strength to keep watch.

A Watchful Eye

1. Does one person make a difference?
2. Can the study of history help us to be God cognizant?
3. Have you been asleep on your watch of liberty?

WATCHWORD
One man with courage makes a majority.

— Andrew Jackson

PRAYER WATCH

Father of Freedom;

We come with heavy hearts.

How easily we have slipped into complacency.

Our silence is a deafening rebuke.

YOUR Word has placed a finger on the pulse of our personal accountability.

Apathy, indifference, passivity to the demise of godliness results in bondage, injustice and loss of liberty.

We must come home or there will not be a home to welcome us.

Forgive us.

Set our feet upon the Rock of the Word.

Call us to stand and intervene.

Stoke our feeble faith until it ignites a fire which reclaims our passion to live for YOU.

Life in our land is seeded in Life with YOU.

Liberty was built on a solid foundation by our forefathers.

Keep us watchful and mindful of the deep Love of God they possessed so that we may consciously uphold those same precious values to the best of our ability.

Liberty must have air to breath and space to grow, generations to be raised up.

We have heard YOU speak from YOUR WORD.

The power of one is the POWER of ONE in YOU.

In Christ alone we shall prevail.

CHAPTER 7

SACRAMENTAL STRENGTH

Be sure God ne'er dooms to waste the strength He deigns to impart.
— Robert Browning

We must learn to live in the Shelter of God.

In it there is unending supply and constant provision for His own.

It is a stored-up strength.

How great is your goodness which you have stored up for those who fear you....[1]

Life with God has goodness stored up for us to partake.

When turmoil enters our lives, we run to Him sometimes in panic because we look at the calamity instead of the surety of the Creator.

He knows we need the Shelter of His Word.

Opening the Bible initially we tentatively start to explore what it says to us. The very act of seeking causes us to find His Resource and so we return again and again to uncover His story, which becomes our story. When we begin to live there we unconsciously draw His life into ours because His life is the Word. In it is the revelation of mankind's search for a King, an

Authority. We take it in and digest it like food. It becomes a part of our very being.

He is there waiting for us.

In its study we find our weakness can be transformed by His strength.

They that wait upon the Lord will renew their strength, they shall mount up with wings as eagles, they shall run and not be weary.... [2]

Then the Bible begins to speak to us personally, powerfully and providentially.

We develop a hunger for it and feel empty without it.

It is comfort, instruction, admonition, warning and fulfillment. Then one day it becomes an outward symbol of our inward Life with God.

It feeds our soul and creates hope.

The Word is sacramental.

Our Love for our Lord grows as we partake His Word and joy erupts in unexpected ways even in crisis.

Our view of the world begins to change because we have looked at it through the lens of His Word. God cognizance brightens our eye and we see possibilities open up where none existed before in people, places, circumstances and challenges.

"The word of God has to anchor itself in the center of our being." [3]

Finally we move into the habit of living in the Word.

It then becomes a shelter, a profound protection encapsulating our potential, peace and position.

The Life of Christ is established in the Word. He creates a place in us where we retreat to worship and search for answers or a place where we are compelled to go out of desperation.

It is a sanctuary God has prepared for us.

Christ *in* me is an amazing concept.

The Bible confirms it for it says, *Christ in me, the hope of glory.*[4]

By His Spirit He lives in believers who have invited Him into their lives by an act of the will, a prayer, an invitation.

But to as many as have received him to them he gave the right to be called the children of God.[5]

Our relationship to God through Jesus is the beginning of Life in the Shelter.

Through Jesus we belong.

The Bible becomes spiritual access to truth and training.

Embracing the Word of God as habit unfolds the sacrament of the Word and equips us to see God in everything.

What is sacramental living?

"To speak of life as 'sacramental' means that everything visible in some way points to the invisible – in Christian understanding.... The sacramental life sees the relational dynamics of life with God invoked in every moment of life. It awakens us to the sacrament of the present moment – whether doing dishes as Brother Lawrence experienced while practicing the presence of God...or reading a short story by Flannery O'Conner, a writer of startling and earthy clarity about spiritual things...or reminding children to pick up their clothes while trying to get laundry put away before leaving for soccer practice; or showing up at work to perform the same tasks carried out yesterday and the day before."[6]

This is faith in action.

Entering into the Shelter of His Word equips us to live out in the world what we learn.

What is the impact of this life style?

"The sacramental allows us to see and receive the gift of God's presence."[7]

We see God in the moment and experience His grace for, "we are grasped from beyond. To the eye and ear everything may seem the same, but in our souls everything is changed."[8]

He becomes transcendent, which means He is connecting the dots in our lives.

It is a bridge we cross in which we glimpse the reality that His knowledge does embrace all we know.

Nothing is incidental.

All is significant.

We are His design.

Then we comprehend with bated breath the dawning reality that His influence and authority is unparalleled, matchless, consummate, unrivaled, predominant.

Strengthened we find our place as His people.

This mystery continues to unfold and His transcendent life is marked out for us.

The shelter of the Word becomes a rich repository of stored strength streaming into ours.

On October 3, 2007, my ill mother passed away after several months of decline with weakened bones, weakened will and a weakened mind. Finally her body shut down. The sustaining power of God's Word became my source of strength. For months I cried out for rest day and night, running into the shelter of His Word.

My watch over her was an assignment to teach me to accept where He had placed me, to persevere, to watch and wait.

He knew the beginning and the end of my watch for He was ever present.

Her frail struggle became mine.

Her holy moment of release was mine.

Her precious peace was mine.

My watch ended.

Exhausted but sustained, my soul was flooded with waves of gratitude and thanksgiving washing over me.

Oh, the faithfulness of God!

For this entire year a group of women from a church in Indiana had been praying for me as I kept them informed about the daily ebb and flow of this time of care-giving for I was scheduled to be with them at a retreat the weekend after my mother died.

They knew that it might not be possible for me to come but they prayed on for me…carrying me.

My family agreed that mother's funeral would be scheduled for the following week for a variety of reasons including the timing and place of her burial and the dialysis schedule of my step-father.

I began to earnestly seek the Lord about going to Indiana.

Would I go?

Should I go?

Could I go?

Yes, I was weary.

Yes, I had been stretched in all ways.

Yes, I was weak.

Several people gave me counsel of all kinds but I knew my Heavenly Father would guide me in His Word and give me peace if I was to go.

I would know what to do.

He did.

Mother was gone.

I had finished my task. Even her eulogy was written. I worked on it for days before she passed away. I wept and worshipped my way through as I wrote early in the mornings for I knew I could not wait until the moment of her death.

It would be too overwhelming to write it and then prepare to deliver it.

Grief zapped my strength.

I had prepared for the retreat throughout the year as snippets of time were seized in my study in the wee hours before most days began.

How I love the Word of God!

So I was ready but I had to have God's will confirmed for me in the Word.

My husband was waiting for me to make the decision. I do not accept commitments anywhere unless he is in agreement for his covering is a shield of safety over me. I prayed, "Show me Lord from the Word if I am to go or stay. Make it clear."

He did.

I found the answer in Psalm 116: 12-14

How can I repay the Lord for all his goodness to me?

I will lift up the cup of salvation and call on the name of the Lord.

I will fulfill my vows to the Lord in the presence of all his people.

Immediately peace came and I knew I was to go.

I packed a bag, boarded a plane and flew there to fellowship in the Word that weekend with a wonderful group of sensitive, loving, women who surrounded me with compassion.

It was a privilege.

Blanketed by His presence I opened my Bible and began to share the marvel of His love with an almost effortless ease. I was completely lifted out of my months of fatigue and strengthened with such grace. I was in awe as I retired to my room to rest that evening. Such thanksgiving welled up within me. I was not alone in this journey for in the months of vigil over my mother He had been doing a new work in me. I had much to learn about serving, keeping watch in love, being accountable, surrendering my will and trusting Him for daily strength.

Abiding in His Word caused my faith to turn the corner to trust and then joy came.

That night as I closed my eyes in sleep I placed my opened Bible on my chest as though its presence being there would infuse me with fresh faith. Truly the Word strengthened me in every way. I was in a quiet place with the silence I craved, sheltered.

The Word of God became sacramental in me.

When the retreat came to a close I expressed my thanks to these dear women. Holding up my Bible I said to them, "You can see that it is all marked up for I have learned to live in this book and so I know you can also, for it will sustain you through all the seasons of life. You know what I have just experienced because you have carried me in prayer. Now I must go home and prepare for the celebration of my mother's home-going. Read, study, live and write in your Bible until you can trace your journey of faith in it. Then retire it and put it aside for God wants to take you to some places you have not been. The familiar must be exchanged for the unknown. Therefore you can observe that I will need to start on a new Bible soon for my faith journey has led me once more to the place of loss. I have much to learn. This I know: He is faithful."

Then as they gathered around me and prayed for my strength, my tears fell for the first time like the gentle rain falling outside the camp. The rustling of the wind was the sound of my first autumn without mother. The trees were letting go of their leaves once more. I, too, had to let go and let God move me upward once again to the rung of steadfast reliance waiting on the ladder of living faith.

"The Bible is not an end in itself, but a means to bring men to an intimate and satisfying knowledge of God, that they may enter into Him, that they may delight in His presence, may taste and know the inner sweetness of the very God Himself in the core and center of their hearts," quotes A. W. Tozier.

Indeed I had.

I flew home completely filled up with strength stored up by the goodness of God for me during this brief but rich respite.

I was supernaturally enabled to pour out and take in at the same time in my weakness and in the coming days I was sustained, secure and stabilized for the Word of God is a shelter.

"When we become a follower of Christ, we become a living sacrament. Our lives in whole become an outward sign of an inward transformation…living each moment as a sacred time to see God's love, power and grace as a reality." [9]

I experienced this phenomenon.

It pleased the Lord for the sake of his righteousness to make his law great and glorious. [10]

As Thanksgiving Day approached, a package came in the mail from this retreat group in Indiana.

It was a gift of strength, a new Bible.

I opened it and with tears of delight began discovering scriptural places of shelter in which to dwell that I will need for my next leg of my journey.

My heart overflowed with deep appreciation for surely the Lord was in our midst that October weekend in the woods.

With God's cognizance I pressed on and so must you.

His Word is a shelter.

Noted Scottish pastor Alexander McClaren solidifies our position in Christ as described in His Word, "Only he who can say, 'the Lord is the strength of my life', can say "of whom shall I be afraid."

Find strength to keep watch.

Live in the shelter.

How great is your goodness, which you have stored up for those who fear you, which you bestow in the sight of men on those who take refuge in you. In the shelter of your presence you hide them from the intrigues of men. [11]

A Watchful Eye

1. How important is the Bible to you?
2. Have you learned to live in it?
3. Is sacramental living beneficial?

Watchword

I am busily engaged in the study of the Bible. I believe it is God's Word because it finds me where I am.

— Abraham Lincoln

Prayer Watch

Generous Father;

YOUR Word is a gift of strength.

So much time I have spent running in other directions.

I was unaware of the storehouse of promises waiting from YOU to show me how to live.

I realize when I ignore YOUR Word, I ignore YOU.

Now I better understand my weakness, my lack of strength.

My diluted life needs shelter.

The foundation of truth must be laid deliberately.

I must live in the Word.

Forgive me.

Jesus I come.

Rebuild the brokenness in me and raise up the Shelter of YOUR Word in my life.

I will go there daily as the world becomes dark and undependable but strengthened again I will go forth to take up my call as a devoted bearer of YOUR LIFE.

Sheltered I will emerge readied to do go where ever YOU lead.

CHAPTER 8

HOLY STRENGTH

What is it that gleams through me, and smites my heart without wounding it? I am both a-shudder and a-glow. A-shudder insofar as I am not like it, a-glow insofar as I am like it.

— St. Augustine

Living in the shelter of God is Holy strength.

He calls us to be holy.

Who may ascend into the hill of the Lord? Or who shall stand in His holy place? He who has clean hands and a pure heart, who has not lifted up his soul unto vanity or sworn deceitfully.[1]

What are God's requirements to commune with Him?

"These verses cover the conduct, motivation, attitude and prioritization of one's life. A deceitful heart will never meet the standards because it does not operate from a foundation of godly integrity."[2]

Clean hands and a pure heart are required.

There cannot be excessive pride, vanity or false witness.

God is holy.

To seek Him, to come to His hill, His holy place, we must be made holy.

Is it possible?

"Holiness is the way to be fully human. Rather than take Jesus at his word, we accept our culture's soft bromide, 'Nobody's perfect.' Yet to use biblical language, to be perfect is to be holy.... We're called to be holy because we are designed to be holy. Mercedes-Benz automobiles are designed to run well – and they do. They're excellent cars. Excellence begins with how high you set your standards. Similarly we were designed to live well, to be persons of integrity. Holiness is our standard, the proper way to be fully human.... C.S. Lewis taught that the singular, eminently attainable goal for which we should strive is holiness: a sincere soul-surrender that unites us with God and the developing virtuous character that results from that union." [3]

It is possible.

Be holy, because I am holy. [4]

Intimacy with God is where it begins.

In fellowship with Him, we are invited to participate.

He doesn't need us to accomplish anything.

He chooses to include us out of love.

The awe of this unconventional alliance: a holy God with an unholy people could only happen because His heart desires to be knitted to ours.

God...has called you into fellowship with his son Jesus Christ our Lord. [5]

He loves to be loved.

Understanding how He longs for us to meet with Him should overwhelmingly draw us to do so.

Prayer is cultivating this relationship.

Since He is holy we must be holy.

The process of seeking Him in prayer is the purest pleasure I know.

This communion could be described like this: A child wants to meet with his Father daily and as he does, love grows and the desire to be like Him evolves. In time anticipation increases as does familiarity, assurance and joy for he loves being in His Father's presence.

Cleans hands and a pure heart are necessary.

We must have them to be in the presence of a Holy God.

At first prayer is more like a check list of careful confessions of our wrongs and a pleading of forgiveness which we discover He delights to give.

Then it changes into a yearning passion to be made ready in order to worship.

Our God checks us when we err, bringing to mind the condition of our hands and hearts. Then it becomes easy for us to identify what makes our hands dirty and our hearts darkened.

Our cleansing through confession is necessary in order to be strengthened for the work at hand.

His Spirit is ever waiting for us to come for we need both love and discipline to be made holy.

His holiness should be a way of life for to be holy is to be set apart for Him, His purposes.

He quickens us to renew our minds constantly and in so doing make visible the invisible through our actions.

Our hearts transform our thought life and guide us into right intentions.

Prayer is a means to call us to holiness.

When we taste of His holiness we are never the same.

He knows motive and priority, conscientiously revealing ours to us.

The question is this: Do we want to learn and commit to intimacy on His terms? If we do we will desire to please Him with holy lives.

God wants me and you...for Himself.

Conceptually, it is astonishing but true.

As we engage in thanksgiving and are drawn into worship, we present an offering.

"In thanksgiving and adoration we come to God not to ask but to give! We come not in whimpering but in shouting praise, not in guilt but gratitude. We feel not distant from God but close to God. We are like a traveler who is home again at last, the prodigal at the banquet. Those moments may be seldom but when they happen we know that we were created *for* God....You leave all that held you bound – money, misery, sin and sickness – leave it behind in doxology."[6]

When this happens you and I have made space for God and gladness comes.

Don't leave home without it.

A Holy God wants to fellowship with us through prayer.

Imagine this?

Fellowship is a shelter.

We can go daily as we respond to His call meet with Him.

This place within becomes a refuge.

"God always meets us where we are and slowly moves us into deeper things. Occasional joggers do not suddenly enter an

Olympic marathon. They prepare and train themselves over a period of time, and so should we."[7]

How do we begin?

Pursue prayer. Look up scriptures on prayer and especially focus on Jesus' prayer life. Study the Lord's Prayer. Read some biographies of men and women of prayer like George Mueller and Amy Carmichael. Look at the lives of E. M. Bounds and Richard Foster. These will validate the quest for the holiness of God and the work of prayer He wants to do in us. Don't substitute reading about prayer for praying.

Practice living in the shelter of prayer.

You will then know what your weaknesses are and will willingly lay them down before your Lord and in so doing take up His Strength. You will relish your time in prayer so much that it becomes a praying life that breathes prayer moment to moment.

We can be holy every day.

Will we succeed every time?

Probably not, but we can start over when we slip into the abyss of self which screams for attention.

He is a watchful, patient, waiting God.

He calls us to be holy.

It is a choice.

It is strength.

When we pursue Him in prayer, we become reformers destined to recover a compromised world that needs to see the power of prayer lived out under the loving authority of a holy God.

We commence by wanting what God wants and our vanities begin to vanish for our pleasure in Him eclipses the temptations we struggle with and our attempts at self promotion.

They die a slow death but they will die when faced with pleasing a Holy God.

As we live in the shelter of prayer we become the shelter of prayer to others.

Our fellowship with God is a treasure to be shared.

He begins with us but it is only the launch.

We run there for ourselves and then we see that our families and friends are a part of our shelter.

He continues to enlarge this shelter and sometimes strangers and aliens are included.

What seemed exclusive becomes inclusive.

We do not pray for everyone in the world.

We pray for those He brings to us.

When I am impressed to pray for a cancer patient, I take them on for life – through chemo, remission, setbacks, respites, family hardships and home going. I pledge to pray for them all the days of their lives.

I do not let go.

Why?

Because I have received my ordained summons from Him.

It is holy help.

How?

Because He supplies the strength and will to do it in us.

How can I refuse?

When someone asks you to pray for them, don't tell them you will and then never begin.

Prayer is perhaps the most selfless act we do and any follower of Christ can enter this shelter.

Carry them and God will carry you.

It is unseen but known by a holy God.

Sometimes there are emergencies…an accident, a job loss, a sick child, a surgery.

Stop and pray.

Be the hands and heart of God in the moment.

There will be natural disasters and calamities of such horror and scale that you may question momentarily if praying will be of any benefit in them. Earthquakes, tornadoes, floods, fires deliver devastating blows but so do kidnappings, crimes of passion, parental abuse, gang violence, robberies, murder. They all obliterate the breath of reason and understanding within us.

We must respond.

Just do it.

Plug holes, build bridges, intercept criminals, connect families, remove danger, bring healing, bless friends, and strengthen your nation in prayer.

"This is the plan for empowering us to be a magnetic presence for God in the world."[8]

Be a prayer shelter.

You will fill the gap in someone's life.

You will discover the more that you give yourself to prayer, the more you comprehend its far reaching impact.

The great surprise is this: the one who prays will be changed the most, which is what God wants to do.

Then there will times you desperately need prayer yourself and others will take you into their shelter.

I remember returning from a speaking trip in Illinois in December 2008. God had blessed my time there even though there were challenges to overcome. I came home depleted but filled up with amazement, for He orchestrates everything when we submit our way to Him. There were women in every place battling brokenness, illness, financial disparity, loneliness, anxiety and fear. The human condition does not exist in a void. I had listened, prayed, shared God's Word and tried to encourage.

As usual when I come home from such a week of pouring out, I need to withdraw and recalibrate…to be quiet and seek the balance of reentry into normal living. It is the daily spiritual habits of our lives privately that equip us to be able to go and do public events in the strength and admonition of the Lord. I love sharing but I understand that my part is to prepare as best I can while at the same time recognizing that unless He goes before me and strengthens me, I can do nothing.

God cognizance is having His perspective and seeking His awareness.

I am dependent upon Him.

False perceptions can sabotage of our efforts.

For me standing before an audience can be entertaining and winsome for God has equipped me with a sense of humor. Just look around at some us and you'll smile…but it is not entertainment for me.

For me it is not performance because technique and training alone will not move the human heart to hear and respond to His truth but partnering in prayer with Him will.

For me it is not a mechanical presentation of what I think but a progression of my faith journey and life experience finely tuned by study in the Word and researched to fit the topical theme required.

It can only be delivered by the power of His strength…only.

Therefore depending on the event's demands, I must go to my prayer shelter seeking His way in order to do anything.

Scripture tells us: *but we have the mind of Christ.*[9]

We are to love the Lord with all our heart, all our strength, all our soul and all our mind.

Loving Him through prayer is one way of seeking His mind in a matter which He will impart to us.

Think on this truth.

We can have the mind of Christ.

This is mind altering.

Knowing this truth and asking for it prepares us to be able to operate in strength and authority.

His success in us is an exhilarating, consuming, work of love.

We are enabled uniquely to serve in the strength which He provides for the task at hand.

It is a heady moment that is too rich for us to live in very long.

When I come home exhausted gloriously, I am coming back to normalcy.

On this trip to Illinois, I returned physically sick.

I do not ever remember arriving home from a speaking experience really ill.

It seemed to be a sore throat at first and so I did the usual herbal remedies, teas and of course prayer. I arrived on Thursday and by Sunday I seemed to be getting worse; therefore, I e-mailed an inner circle of special praying friends asking them to intercede for me. My discomfort was increasing with sinus pressure, and Monday morning I knew I was headed to the doctor's office because my throat was burning. After an ultrasound of my sinuses and chest the doctor said, "You are very sick with sinus infection and bronchitis." When he examined my throat he jokingly asked me if I had been drinking battery acid for I had developed hives inside, which is not a laughing matter. A shot in the hip and antibiotics for seven days was ordered, along with some other meds to help me begin to recover. Yes, I was crying out to God for relief and so were many others. Never once did I let go of the belief that He would prevail and yet the odds kept escalating me toward crisis. I entered a critical stage late that night. I could not swallow without a fiery pain. I did not want to swallow. My throat felt raw, exposed and enflamed. I realized the hives could swell together obstructing the passageway.

Fear started closing in on me.

Just trying to drink water, which I needed to stay hydrated, was impossible for it ignited my throat like alcohol on an open wound…an unquenchable burning. I was in a dark tunnel of helplessness and weakness. My misery index was over the top for I was unable to swallow – period. At one point my husband,

Roy, thought he was going to have to call 911. Then suddenly a window of clarity opened in my mind and I knew what I needed. Roy must pray out loud over me. This was the breakthrough. If he did not I was on my way to the hospital. I asked him to do so and I will never forget as long as I live how lovingly he took my hand and began to ask God to intervene for me, to come and touch my throat. The sound of my husband's strong gentle voice in prayer is a memory I will carry with me forever. With a holy finality he said, "Billie, go to sleep now for you are going to be better in the morning."

I did and I was.

Awakening at about 4:30 am I got up and stayed up in prayer and thanksgiving to my God, surrendering many things again to Him, pledging my love for I knew my crisis had peaked. Scriptures came to me from Isaiah 30:15: *In quietness and confidence is my strength* and in Job 13:15 the words *though He slay me yet will I trust in Him*.

My God responded to my husband's prayer.

I felt a-shudder and a-glow.

I could swallow.

By 9 am I swallowed oatmeal without pain.

God answered my husband's prayer.

Prayer is a shelter in which we learn the holiness of God.

God teaches us to live there.

Sometimes we are the shelter to another and sometimes we are carried there by someone else.

It is a place of holy strength.

Call on His Name and get to know Him.

Find strength to keep watch.

Live in the shelter.

How great is your goodness which you have stored up for those who fear you, which you bestow in the sight of men who take refuge in you. In the shelter of your presence you hide them from the intrigues of men.[10]

A Watchful Eye

1. Does a holy God desire fellowship with us?
2. Can a praying life become a shelter for others?
3. How does His strength become ours?

Watchword
Standeth God in the shadow keeping watch over his own.

— James Russell Lowell

Prayer Watch
Guardian Father;

Can our lives be so integrated with YOU that the flow of YOUR strength becomes ours?

Can it be that YOUR longing for fellowship with us is the holy nudge we feel when we bow our heads in prayer?

Trained to trust we will not despair.

Can we seek the mind of Christ and know He will bring His mind to us in all matters if we ask?

Holy lives will be the requirement.

Ever Watchful Father we believe the answers are yes, yes and yes for YOU are holy, holy, holy.

We are called to be holy.

Show us how to comprehend holiness in the practical as we bow seeking YOUR grace.

Prepare a place within us and call us there daily.

With joy or sadness, trouble or triumph, we'll become a people of prayer.

Shelter us so we may shelter others.

Forgive us for prayerlessness.

Forgive us for absent fellowship.

Forgive us for unholy living.

Receive our abundant love we pray in Jesus' Name.

CHAPTER 9

ENCOMPASSED STRENGTH

My joy, my grief, my hope, my love, Did all within this circle move.
— Edmund Waller

Living in the shelter of God is encompassed strength.

He sets boundaries for our day, our lives, our seasons, our times.

Encompassed means surrounded, encircled, enfolded, and enveloped.

What surrounds us daily?

Troubles without number surround us.[1]

We need His circle of strength.

God is our refuge and strength, an ever present help in trouble.[2]

He has called us together in community to be strength to one another.

A new commandment I give to you. Love one another as I have loved you.[3]

Loving one another enlarges the family circle.

Live in harmony with one another.[4]

Living in harmony with one another strengthens the family ties of love in Him.

Accept one another, then, as Christ accepted you in order to bring praise to God.[5]

Accepting one another is the role of the family of God.

Carry each other's burdens, and in this way you will fulfill the law of Christ.[6]

Carrying one another's burdens is the mentoring of faith.

What a picture of being encompassed by the love of God… the circle of one another.

What fellowship we gather as we reach out to one another and become a circle of strength.

We uncover the extraordinary love of God for one another at the Brooklyn Tabernacle Church in New York City.

Pastor, author Jim Cymbala and six-time Grammy winning choir director wife Carol Cymbala have been there for 25 years bringing the life of Christ to the inner city. They began with a broken down facility and a handful of people. It seemed a task too big to undertake.

It was, but not for God.

He preached.

She led music.

Carol had just a few people interested in singing in the choir at first but God had put Jim and Carol together as a team. People who were in search of a shelter of love began to attend this church. The ministry to one another began to swell for Brooklyn Tabernacle became known as a house of continuous prayer. The doors opened and the people came. In 1980 Carol began to look for music for the choir. As men and women found their way to this Shelter of God's love, they found the Jesus who loved them and HE began to change them. As real faith flourished in these lives, it reproduced itself by encountering others who needed rescue and strength for the journey.

The circle widened.

"God is always present. He calls us to be his life in this world, to serve with abandon, joy and love. We must be ready to serve." [7]

The choir formed. It became an encompassing presence of faith. Rehearsals began and ended in prayer. Carol, who could neither read nor write music, directed and wrote their music. A mighty movement of God's sacramental music began to sweep across New York City and soon the nation. In a short while these untrained voices were enjoined into a company of 285. They performed, recorded and toured all over the nation and overseas. As they sang the blessing of God came down for their music was His. Pastor Cymbala describes his church this way, "It is a mixture of ethnic, economic backgrounds; attorneys, former street people, nurses and ex crack addicts....You name it and we have someone who has been saved out of it standing right next to someone who has grown up in the church." [8] The choir sang and moved as one in passion, joy and hope.

One cannot hear them without joining them in worship. It is the Voice of the wounded, restored and strengthened by the Healer, Jesus.

Stories of the choir abound.

A stunning African-American woman who looks to be in her twenties shared her journey of faith on their web site.

Her name is Jasmeen.

It is a crushing beginning for this endearing young woman with bright eyes and a contagious smile. She was raised solely by her grandmother who stood in for both parents who were absent. In her child-like way she believed grandmother to be her mother while growing up until a cruel classmate told her, "At least I have a mother." Only then did she learn the truth.

There were many missing spaces in her life.

Jasmeen's father, a drug addict, who abused her mother, had struck a fatal blow ending her mother's life and for this crime he was imprisoned.

Therefore she was motherless forever and seemingly fatherless as well.

With anguish she describes her hatred for him upon learning about the details of her mother's death.

"I do not want to have any relationship with the man who would take my mother's life."

Her search for love drew her down dark streets of night life into clubs and the partying scene. Living a double life, she hid her secret behavior from grandmother but it began to take a toll. Desperate for answers, she found her way to a community gathering where a woman spoke about Brooklyn Tabernacle's amazing choir. Jasmeen found herself surrounded by people who were warm and accepting.

They welcomed her with the love of Christ.

She was invited to go and hear the choir and when she did, she entered the Shelter of God's love.

Much emotional homework was still ahead for her. There was anger and bitterness toward this errant, criminal father. He had been in prison for 23 years with no contact. Miraculously, one day after much thought, she had a desire to write him a letter and when she did, he answered.

Letters were exchanged for two years and affirmations of love began to flow between them.

Words written down on paper that could be read again and again began to fill up some of those empty years and she finally began to call him Father. In her own words she said, "I started to love him." God's Love in her caused her to forgive her father.[9]

Only the love of God can break the cycle of hatred.

Today God's encompassing love is still transforming her life and Jasmeen is giving back to the community by meeting with a local youth group to encourage them to find their way to the Shelter of God's Love.

Touched by her story I went to their web site again and listened to the choir perform the music, *I'm Amazed That You Love Me.*

God's music brings us to the shelter of love.

Seated at my desk and watching intently I was mesmerized by voices lifted to God and I joined in their praise. I looked into the animated faces of a multinational choir representing the world and they sang with a holy fervor and conviction. The indwelling Christ who had redeemed them was given away as an offering in song to any who would stop and receive.

I received.

In fact, I had to stand up from the computer and lift my hands to my Father in worship for I was encompassed by His love for me. This choir truly embodies the presence of God when they sing and when we receive His Love, we are strengthened.

My day's long hours of tension at the computer dissipated for my heart was overflowing with more of Him and less of me.

It caused me to long to hear them sing in person and yearn to sing in a choir like that one day.

In March 2008, I was a part of an event in Memphis, Tennessee called "Redemption."

Two best friends, Ellen Olford, a Caucasian women's ministry director and Priscilla Shirer, a gifted African-American speaker/author met and began to seek God about a gathering for our city that would bring together women from different socio-economic backgrounds and denominations which would be representative of areas surrounding our city. They wanted to reach out to all women and draw them into a circle of God's love. The planning encompassed about three and one half years. Prayer was the foundation. A team was assembled and a launch to include as many churches as possible was underway. Pivotal leaders were scattered throughout the city and its suburbs. Prayer meetings weekly fortified our teams. Visits to churches proceeded. Relationships were forming. We were becoming an army of women on mission.

Our city needs racial healing.

We need walls that divide people to be replaced with community.

We need friendships with one another.

We need to move out of comfortable "churchianity" into the reality of Life with God which changes us.

A call to revival was coming.

Cook Convention Center, downtown Memphis, was chosen as our meeting place.

A budget had to be assembled and prayed through.

Would we?

Could we?

Would He?

Ellen was the driving force and Priscilla was the messenger.

Months passed.

Prevailing prayer continued.

Money came in and churches were added.

A web site was established.

I wrote prayers for the web to encourage women to come and find the Love of God through Jesus.

Finally the weekend arrived.

350 churches participated.

The budget was met.

I was privileged to sing in the multiracial choir that moved with one voice for One Audience.

When I looked out on the audience of 9,000 women, I was encompassed with the greatness of a loving God who would gather us together enlarging the Shelter of His love.

We sang the music *God of the City* as a video flashed images on the overhead screens of our downtown; tall buildings, the Mississippi River, Beale Street, restaurants, bars, people searching for meaning in all the wrong places.

Together we cried out to God for our city and He heard our cries.

This was the truest corporate worship I have ever experienced. I will never forget.

We were united through prayer and we became God cognizant through action.

The Bible was opened and we were taught how to live and move and have our being in Christ Jesus.

When Truth is proclaimed, the Christ of scripture is made known and the Cross of sacrifice is lifted up.

Broken lives are made whole.

It happened.

Encompassed by His love our circle of strength encircled the city.

We pledged to find a prayer partner and forge a relationship of intimacy and love meeting together monthly with someone located in another area of the city…to keep watch over another.

We did.

It is a ministry called Two by Two.

My partner is Jada, an energetic, innovative, charming African-American woman in ministry making a difference in this city while also working on a PhD in education.

She is now a single mother with a grown son in the military.

We have enlarged our circle of friendship by including one another.

This incredible event opened a door that needs to reach across our nation and the world.

Beginnings require a watch.

God is strengthening His people by surrounding them with a large and diverse family that will stand shoulder to shoulder and hand in hand enfolded into the lives of one another.

We are a family of faith.

The things that we love tell us who we are.

— Thomas Aquinas

God's love is a shelter of encompassed strength.

Home is a shelter where the circle of love waits.

Find strength to keep watch.

Live in the Shelter.

How great is your goodness, which you have stored up for those who fear you, which you bestow on those who take refuge in you. In the shelter of your presence you hide them from the intrigues of men. [10]

A WATCHFUL EYE

1. Is there a circle of faith that encompasses your life?

2. Is God calling you to move out of your comfort zone and join His plans to enlarge your circle?

3. Does the ministry of one another work through you?

WATCHWORD
Our life is an apprenticeship to the truth that around every circle another can be drawn. Every end is a beginning.

— Ralph Waldo Emerson

PRAYER WATCH

Encompassing Father;

YOU surround us with YOUR Love.

YOUR people woo us to strength through love.

YOU are the One who hears our prayer for unity.

Make us one in YOU.

Bind us with chords which cannot be broken.

Knit us together under the Cross.

Fill us with more love and expectancy.

Call us to worship.

Turn our life experience into praise for YOU.

Blend our lives and birth a people free from prejudice and pride.

Move us through impossibilities and envelop us with YOUR love.

Our world will change then.

We must become the circle that is centered in Life with God, ever present and willing to include another.

Come, we pray, and encompass our lives with YOUR Strength.

The days of weakness will come, but in Jesus' Name we shall overcome together.

CHAPTER 10

LUMINOUS STRENGTH

Come forth into the Light of Things.

— William Wordsworth

Living in the shelter of God brings luminous strength.

God is light. In Him there is no darkness at all. If we walk in the light as He is in the light we have fellowship one with another, and the blood of Jesus cleanses us from all sin.[1]

The Word of God tells us that in God there is no darkness.

None at all.

He is Light.

Then we learn that if we will walk in this light, we will have fellowship with each other.

Fellowship forever.

Next we are reminded that it is the blood of Jesus' sacrifice for our sin that brings us access to God.

Relationship to God.

This is union with God.

Union gives strength.

— Aesop

His light is found in His Word and internalizing it personally brings sacramental living that shines.

Fellowship with Him in prayer and exploring His holiness creates intimacy.

In coming together with other believers and learning to love one another, the body of Christ is formed.

Choosing to live in His Light strengthens.

What is natural light?

Scientifically it is a study of properties, energy and nature's resources.

"Light is a form of radiant energy that you can detect with your eyes…. It is a combination of electrical and magnetic energy that travels very, very fast…approximately 300,000 km per second. There are two types of light: luminous objects that emit their own light (the sun) and non-luminous objects that do not emit light (a flashlight that is switched off). Light is made up of photons, very small particles of energy. It travels in straight lines but in small waves. An example would be tossing a pebble into a pond. The ripples produced (small waves) travel in a straight line away from the source, the pebble…. Luminous light from fluorescence is the process of emitting light while receiving energy from another source and luminous light from phosphorescence is the process of emitting light for sometime after receiving energy form another source." [2]

And God is Light.

He is strength.

Luminous is defined as emitting light, full of light, resplendent, aflame, incandescent, lustrous, aglow, radiant.

Light in us is a reflection of His Light for He is the source.

Even when we are surrounded by darkness He provides light.

Even in darkness light dawns for the upright, gracious, compassionate man.[3]

The precepts of the Lord are right, giving joy to the heart. The commands of the Lord are radiant, giving light to the eyes.[4]

Living His precepts brings energy and insight for it is truth.

Send forth your light and your truth, let them guide me; let them bring me to your holy mountain, to the place where you dwell.[5]

How does His Light mirror luminous strength?

Nature provides a glimmer.

Scientists have brought to light a fresh prospectus on how mother-of-pearl, or nacre is formed, using the polarized x-ray beams and nanoscale imaging of Berkeley Lab's Advanced Light Source.

In layman's terms, they have studied the process under advanced light technology.

Mother of pearl, iridescent in beauty, is found in the lining of the shells of abalone, mussels and certain other mollusks. It is renowned for amazing strength and toughness that has been a long-standing mystery. Physics professor Pup Gilbert at the University of Wisconsin-Madison has led the research. "Nacre is a biomineral composed of thin layers of crystalline aragonite tablets separated by even thinner layers of organic materials.... This unique structural arrangement was a surprise and could play a role in nacre's remarkable resistance to fracture."[6]

Aragonite layers and something else known as organic layers are bonded together.

"Nacre is a hard biological tissue found in the inner layer of some sea shells such as oyster or abalone. It is a composite material mainly composed of an aragonite phase (95% vol) arranged in micro tablets, bonded together by a biopolymer mortar.... By the addition of a small amount of organic, well designed microstructure nacre achieves strength and toughness."[7]

Our deduction in plain language is this: The inner linings of shells such as Mother-of-pearl are of exceptional strength because of the bonding of two distinct materials, aragonite and mortar.

This design is strength from layers bonded together from the inside out.

When natural light is reflected from the luminous shell called mother-of-pearl, we are mesmerized at the prism of colors intricately interwoven in myriads of shades: soft aqua, rosy pink, amethyst mauve, lustrous green, incandescent gold flowing in a unique design, which displays the handiwork of The Artisan Creator.

Surely this pictures luminous strength.

Beauty and strength bonded.

All of creation reveals God's Light.

So do we.

God chose us.

He invites us to bond with Him through Jesus.

"More of Jesus, More Light, More of me, more confusion. I need His presence every day."[8]

United with Him we are bonded in strength.

Union births strength.

Light shines.

The path of the righteous is like the first gleam of dawn shining till the full light of day. [9]

When living in His Light we embrace God cognizance in all that surrounds us. We can see how nature reveals His intricacies of strength. It is also parallels our human condition.

In 2005, a sports writer for *Sports illustrated named* Rick Reilly wrote an article entitled, *The World's Strongest Dad*. It was based on the inspiring father and son duo, Dick and Rick Hoyt. Dick is a retired Lt. Colonel in the Air National Guard. In 1962, his son Rick was born and diagnosed as a spastic quadriplegic, cerebral palsy, non speaking person. His parents were told to take him home and place him in an institution for he would be a vegetable for the rest of his life.

The parents refused.

They could see that he was keenly aware of their presence for his eyes followed them when they were in a room. By age 11 they decided to take him to Tufts University to see if there might be a way this disadvantaged son could communicate. Dick was told, "No way, for there is nothing going on in his brain." Then Dick asked people who examined him to tell Rick a joke. They did so and Rick laughed. "Turns out a lot was going on in his brain. He was then rigged up with a computer that allowed him to communicate by controlling a cursor which would touch a switch with the side of his head. Rick was finally able to communicate. First words? "Go Bruins!" After a classmate was paralyzed in an accident and the school organized a charity run for him, Rick pecked out on the computer, "Dad I want to do that."[10]

The father who had never run more than a mile was now challenged to run 5 miles pushing a son in a wheelchair.

Could he?

He did and when Rick typed these words, "Dad, when we were running it felt like I wasn't disabled anymore," their lives changed.[11]

They changed course and possibility became reality.

Dick began to work out and got in shape to run the 1979 Boston Marathon.

Because they were not designated as a wheelchair competitor or as a single runner they were ignored by officials but they ran anyway and continued to improve in speed until they were officially qualified to run in the 1983 Boston Marathon.

A friend suggested they try a triathlon.

Dick Hoyt had never learned to swim and had not ridden a bike since he was a boy.

How in the world could he expect to do both and carry a 110 pound kid?

Impossible?

Not for Dick.

To date they have done "212 triathlons, including 4 grueling 15-hour Ironmans in Hawaii. It must be a buzz kill to be a 25 year old athlete getting passed by an old guy towing a grown man in a dinghy."[12]

Why does Dick do this?

He does it to see Rick's face with the cantaloupe smile break across it as they run, swim and ride together.

Father and son have bonded in strength.

In the 1990's Dick suffered a mild heart attack and doctors told him that he probably survived it because he was in such good physical condition.

In a way Rick saved Dick's life.

Father and son, son and father operated together for the benefit of the other.

The bonding of strength overcomes.

Today they are still a team.

Rick is a graduate of Boston University and works with computers. Dad is a motivational speaker. More about their lives can be found at www.teamhoyt.com.

Just watch any video of them competing and absorb the intensity of their arduous tasks through the searching eye of Rick who is locked into a body that does not work. Then observe the progress as competition begins and strength and energy are demanded in the father's legs and arms. When the light of triumph is released in Rick's face and his arm is raised in victory, you will find yourself strengthened.

It is aglow with luminous, shining strength.

Their story strengthens us.

We will need bonded strength for the days ahead.

Anxiety accompanied by disappointment, doubt and delay will knock.

When bills mount, health deteriorates, expectancy nose dives, weakness comes.

My heart pounds, my strength fails me, even the light has gone from my eyes.[13]

Fractured faith will call for splints and perhaps a cast.

We must seek God's Light.

You O Lord keep my lamp burning, my God turns my darkness into light.[14]

His Light is Shelter.

Come to the Shelter.

In your light we see light.[15]

Find strength to keep watch.

Illumined, strengthened, our hearts are warmed and willed for the step ahead.

Radiant words discovered on the Breastplate of St. Patrick:

Christ be my light to illumine and guide me!

Christ be my shield to cover and guard me!

Christ be under me, Christ be over me,

Christ beside me, left and right!

Christ before me, behind me, about me,

Christ this day, within, without me!

Christ in every heart that thinks of me,

Christ in every mouth that speaks to me!

Christ in every eye that sees me,

Christ in every ear that hears!

The Lord is God and he has made his light shine upon us.[16]

The light of the righteous shines brightly.[17]

Life with God shines.

Find strength to keep watch.

Live in the Shelter.

> *How great is your goodness, which you have stored up for those who fear you, which you bestow in the sight of men on those who take refuge in you. In the shelter of your presence, you hide them from the intrigues of men.* [18]

A Watchful Eye

1. Does the darkness of the world extinguish God's Light?
2. In what ways can we contribute to His Light?
3. Will there be enough strength for the tasks ahead?

Watchword

Words which do not give the light of Christ increase the darkness.

— Mother Teresa

Prayer Watch

Radiant Father;

Who knows the shadows of our lives, we bow down.

Darkness is a part of living but it is not a campground.

As surely as the sun rises so does the strength YOU create within us.

When we choose to bond intentionally with YOU, all of life is illumined.

When we leave the presence of YOUR Light, we are weakened.

When we seek to enlarge our vision through the Word, our faith brightens.

The light of the righteous shines brightly but the lamp of the wicked is snuffed out. [19]

Abandoned to our own resources we too are snuffed out.

Forgive us.

Restore our sight for in so doing,

Strengthened we'll stand.

Sustained we'll carry others.

Submitted to Truth, YOUR LIGHT will prevail.

Shine down upon our hearts with a strength that will glow outside them.

In blessed union with Christ Jesus, we pray.

CHAPTER 11

TRANSCENDENT STRENGTH

Gratitude bestows reverence allowing us to encounter every day epiphanies, Those transcendent moments of awe that change forever how we experience life and the world forever.

— John Milton

Living in the shelter of God brings transcendent strength.

Faith encompasses all we are and welcomes all that God is.

"Faith unites, belief divides;

Beliefs are diverse; faith is one;

Faith is objective; belief subjective;

Beliefs are symbolic, faith transcendent;

Faith is personal; beliefs propositional;

Beliefs are historical; Faith is permanent;

Faith is God-given; beliefs community- made;

Beliefs are theoretical; Faith is practical." [1]

"Religious faith is transcendent…it is God in the world, a universal reality. We live in a world of grace…. Every human being is called by God to communion with God in this life and eterndity…called by an inner instinct from God drawing us to belief." [2]

God draws us to Himself.

He made a way for us through the sacrifice of Jesus.

His Perfection was exchanged for our imperfection.

Our sin was covered by the blood of the Sinless One.

We are accepted by a loving God through Christ alone.

But to as many as have received Him to them he gave the right to become children of God.[3]

Our life joins His.

We begin to live with expectancy in Him.

We were made by God for God.

Transcendent is defined as pre–eminent, surpassing all, exalted.

"He is above, beyond and outside all that He created. Belief in His transcendence produces awe, reverence and humility."[4]

He is outside all He has made,

But He is also inside all He has made.

"Nothing could continue to exist for a moment if He were not continually keeping it in being."[5]

Our God is in everything that surrounds us and all that is created in us.

Life with God inspires us to be and do.

We have an outside inside God who invites us to receive all He has stored up for us.

Transcendent moments come.

We are bearers of His life.

Commit your actions to the Lord and your thought will be established.[6]

Early in 2009 my husband Roy and I were privileged to board a ship on a holiday headed for the Southern Caribbean. It was a time set aside to be restored physically, emotionally and spiritually. Life has rhythms which bring balance. Getting out of balance is easy. We planned for a year looking toward this time of retreat and rest. Believing this was a provision of God for us, we eagerly embraced it and were excited about all it might present. I prayed that our God would choose our encounters with people. There are many who need encouragement and sometimes they are specifically placed along our path.

Respite plus faith is strength.

God's strength is transcendent.

Life with God is Life *in* God.

He transcends all.

Our first couple of days found us adjusting to shipboard routine and learning our way around the ship. Getting settled into our quarters we met a very pleasant team of stewards who would be responsible for them. We had Maria from the Philippines and Juan from Puerto Rico. They were always in the hallway working diligently. Both are representative of an international community of workers who contract to work for several months. The hours are long and they are away from home but the financial incentives drive the work. Everywhere there were industrious, outgoing people whose main goal is customer satisfaction. Ciele from India and Daniella from Italy were a concierge team who made reservations for meals, tours and handled calamities. They were seemingly always on duty waiting to assist. The turnover of guests is usually 7-9 days. Imagine what kind of strength and energy is required to be ready to meet, greet and serve others with a constant turnover.

This is more than a game face.

It is a way to live.

Taking my first morning walk was pure delight. As I walked I prayed, "Lord, guide our steps. This is YOUR day. YOU provided this trip. YOU are hovering in the heavens above us but YOU are also right here in our midst. Draw someone today to YOUR LOVE."

Then as I sat down wrapped up in the beauty of the ocean's invitation with my Bible in my lap, I drank in its strength, savoring the words of scripture as I wrote down thoughts I received. Time in God's presence brings God cognizance and we then carry it in us. Praise and thanksgiving overflowed as I gratefully acknowledged my utter dependence upon Him. Worship came. My stillness produced reverence once again for His permeating love and mysterious ways.

The one who calls you is faithful and He will do it.[6]

His word confirms our call and reminds us of our ever present plenitude.

In quiet and confidence is our strength.[7]

Being hushed before Him renews purpose and strengthens resiliency.

He is our Keeper, our Shelter.

Strengthened from the inside we are enabled to enjoy, observe and connect with others by carrying His Life to them. On the second day Roy and I visited the art gallery after dinner. It was a formal night aboard the ship so my husband was dressed in his Navy Dinner Dress Blue uniform complete with ribbons and medals. It is the Navy equivalent of a tuxedo. There we met three young men in their 20's who worked together in the art gallery. Trev, an American from Texas, was immediately drawn to the uniform and began to ask questions about Roy's career. He was the art director. Within minutes he and Roy were carrying on as a father and son might do, joking and teasing about what he missed about home. It was a great connection. Trev had a background in the Air Force and possessed a disarming wit, an engaging way with people. These qualities served him well in his job as art director. We both inquired about his family back in the states and, very candidly, he discussed them with animation except when he mentioned his mother. Tentatively he said "Yes, I have a mother but I haven't spoken to her in a long time."

When I heard that, I made a mental note of that declaration and filed it away.

Roy continued to visit with him and then I turned toward the second young man who had heard the conversation with Trev. They were art associates – Ett, a South African, was a robust looking young man with reddish hair, an appeasing face and charming crisp dialect. I said to him, "Sometimes our mothers can be difficult but they are ours. They gave us life. I am thankful mine was a praying mother."

Bingo!

Ett said, "Did you say you had a praying mother?"

I answered, "Yes, I did."

His face began to brighten as he replied, "I also have a praying mother."

Immediately I seized the moment and asked, "Are you a believer?"

He confirmed, "I am."

Instant connection.

For several minutes he shared his faith and how his new job on the ship in art had come to be. His mother was praying him through. He and I were enjoying the blessing of being in God's family and knowing it. Ett also began to share some of the difficulties of life on a ship.

I listened for insight where encouragement was needed.

He needed fellowship.

It is true that iron sharpens iron.

Trev and Roy had been watching our obvious enthusiasm and Roy interjected, "Honey, are you about ready to go?'

I said, "Not yet, I am visiting with my new brother in Christ."

Roy responded with a hearty "Alright," and shook his hand.

Trev spontaneously said, "Hey, I'm one too." and then showed me a special medal with scripture that he wore around his neck.

In that instant we bonded.

Ogy was the third young man of the trio and he hailed from Serbia. Seated quietly at a desk working as we all dialogued, he flashed an interested look now and then. He seemed more introverted in conversation but keenly observant. His dark hair framed an inquisitive countenance. Ogy's role was to do all the background setup for auctions, access inventory on computer and then prep for the framing of art sold. We met him briefly in passing as we prepared to leave, giving our promise to see them all again at the art events.

God had opened a door and we walked through it.

A transcendent God was at work strengthening us to be His people.

As the days unfolded, it was Ett we seemed to be running into in between the art shows.

He passed by us at lunch one day and we invited him to join us and visit. He had only been aboard a few weeks and was fast assimilating how to live. There were feelings of isolation along with a lack of acceptance. His faith needed revitalizing. Ett needed to create a space for God.

One has to make space.

I challenged him to get up early and go find a spot somewhere on this enormous ship and sit in the presence of the Lord, reading the Word and seeking guidance for practical solutions to daily life.

"Ett, God's life is in you and it is strengthened through the Word. Go there."

He promised he would.

It was just a push upward for a young man who was trying to figure out how to feed his faith in a provocative ever changing environment.

The next time we saw him he was flying around at the auction tagging art to be presented. He came over to me and said, "Mrs. Cash, I did it. I found a spot and I have asked God to bless this day with 50 people who will come to our presentation. In faith I have set up 50 chairs." I smiled and said, "That's faith based on God's provision. You had faith because you had time to seek Him."

He had faith.

He was the leader of the artful three musketeers.

Fifty people came.

Trev was charming, humorous, and knowledgeable and the audience loved him.

We had a delightful time attending these gatherings; experiencing genres of art crossing the centuries, learning about the Great Masters' lives and painting styles but also absorbing the works of well known contemporaries like Peter Max and other innovative artists.

We enjoyed the people who came.

One evening we stopped by the gallery after dinner once again to say hello to the tireless team and to look specifically at the work of Peter Max. He paints images symbolic of our heritage as Americans; the flag, and Lady Liberty. They are fascinating and deeply stirring.

Again I spoke to Ett who informed me confidentially that Ogy was not a Christian but had a girlfriend who was.

I met her later on.

What a God-orchestrated influence to find aboard a ship in the middle of an ocean.

I shared with Ett how much I loved to encourage others to find faith in Christ. I then told him that I write small books which are signposts to Christian living. He pounced on this and said, "Do you have any with you?"

I remarked, "Yes, I do and I plan to give each of you a book before we leave."

He grabbed my hand instantly and thanked me graciously like a son to his mother.

I knew I would be giving them my book, *A Pillow on the Highway.*

They all needed a pillow on the ocean's highway.

Ett need his to remember to trust and rest in God.

Trev needed to release his expectations unto to God.

Ogy needed to find his pillow, His Life in God.

"We are incomplete by ourselves. We can't make anyone love us…. Fulfillment is in God alone. On our own we scheme and dream, faint and fall…. In honoring God we please Him. In pleasing Him, we find rest. It is the pillow of sufficiency."[8]

I noticed that Roy was talking to Trev again and this time he hugged him as we walked away as a father would.

Our time flew by and the last day came.

I felt led to write personal notes to these young men placing them in the books I would leave behind.

I gave them out in the afternoon at the end of the wrap up art event.

Since I did not see Ogy, Ett promised to give him the book.

In Trev's note, I encouraged him to forgive his mother and move on, for unforgiveness blocks blessing and destroys worship. Estrangement shuts down hope.

In Ett's note, I rejoiced in his faith and encouraged him to lead from strength found in the Word and lived out purposely in daily life.

In Ogy's note, I asked him to read the book and consider the Christian life for God calls each of us. I signed my name and the scriptural reference Jeremiah 6:16.

They thanked me and in the evening as we went by the gallery to say goodbye, Trev wanted to take some photos with us.

All three gathered around and we chronicled our adventure together with the camera.

Hugs and well wishes were exchanged with all.

Trev said, "Mrs. Cash I read your note. I promise I will do what you suggested." And then he kissed me on the cheek like a son.

Ett beamed and gave me a note, taking my hand and planting a kiss upon it saying, "May God Bless you everywhere you go. He sent you here."

Ogy smiled and said, "Thank you for the book. I will read it."

As I walked away, Ett ran to me and said, "Mrs. Cash I have got to tell you what Ogy said when I gave him your book this afternoon. He looked at the scripture Jeremiah 6:16 written as an inscription inside his book and said, "I think this must be a sign for me because I was born June 16 (6:16)…God wants me. I will read this book."

Ett handed me a stick 'em memo note thanking God for sending me along his path.

Mothering and Fathering had taken place by a transcendent God who strengthens us to strengthen others.

When we encounter others what will we leave behind?

Spiritual doubt stalked the life of author, poet, teacher Leo Tolstoy.

The excesses of his youth troubled him and yet were a part of his search for meaning. He was privileged in society and considered to be revered as a teacher. He concluded that that one should live his life and find a way to provide the best he could for his family. So with this practical logic he pursued notoriety, wealth, and status. The more successful he became outwardly, the more he questioned the lack of meaning in his life.

Torment descended so swiftly upon him that he soon enjoyed nothing. His life plummeted into despair. "What will come of what I am doing today or shall do tomorrow? What will come of my whole life? Is there any meaning in life that the inevitable death awaiting me does not destroy?"[9]

He explored science, reasoning, math and the lives of intellectual thinkers but still found no satisfying answers. There were religious people in his learned academic circle but he was repelled by their hypocrisy in living. His search led him to identify with Solomon's indictment of the vanity of life.

Then a perception broke through.

"I began to draw near to the believers among the poor, simple lettered folks: pilgrims, monks, sectarians and peasants…. These endlessly different in their manners, minds, education, and position, as they were – all alike. In complete contrast to my ignorance, they knew the meaning of life and death, labored quietly, endured deprivations and sufferings, lived and died, seeing therein not vanity but good…and I learnt to love these people."[10]

Did his love for them enlighten his understanding so that real faith could be seen?

It seems it did.

Did he arrive there?

After studying his life through his book *A Confession*, I find that confusion and misunderstanding still remained but were punctuated by lucid moments of God drawing him.

Only God knows.

The Bible tells us *if you seek me with all your heart you will find me.*[11]

There is a legitimate search for God.

There is a moment when we know we have found our way to Him, a transcendent break through.

In Him we live and move and our being.[12]

This knowledge is grounded in devotion not doubt and with it our journey of faith becomes a trail of triumph in adversity, a tryst of truth in debate, a tender tale of love woven in humility and mercy.

This is Life in the Shelter of transcendent strength.

Strengthened to seek, gratitude births wonder.

God is wonder.

Strengthened to serve, insight frames awe.

God is awe.

An outside inside God is watching.

Find strength to keep watch.

Live in the Shelter.

How great is your goodness, which you have stored up for those who fear you, which you bestow in the sight of men on those who take refuge in you. In the shelter of your presence you hide them from the intrigues of men.[13]

A WATCHFUL EYE

1. Can you grasp the concept that God's knowledge encompasses all things transcending people, place, time and circumstance?

2. Has there been an opportunity in which you were keenly aware you were a part of bringing His life to a stranger?

3. How does personal spiritual discipline reestablish the rhythms of your life physically and emotionally when there is imbalance?

WATCHWORD
Teach me my God and King in all things Thee to see, And what I do in anything, to do it as for Thee.

— George Herbert

PRAYER WATCH

Glorious Father;

Mystery surrounds YOU but does not shroud YOUR Love.

There is a path to Truth.

YOU call us to search for it.

YOUR Word brings strength.

YOU beckon us to prayer.

In YOUR presence we find refuge.

Everywhere we go YOU have been.

Everywhere we are YOU are.

Everywhere we plan to go YOU are waiting.

YOUR Life within us is Life.

It is abundant and abiding.

Keep us seeking and risking.

Stir us to foster faith.

Give us grateful hearts that yearn to experience more of YOU.

Intercept us with others who need a spiritual transfusion of hope.

The miraculous abounds when our eyes are opened to see and our ears are tuned to hear.

YOUR WORD prepares us to give where ever we find someone searching.

Strengthened, we rejoice in YOUR Providence knitting us together with neighbors, friends and strangers.

How lavish is YOUR Love which connects us and makes us one Indeed YOU transcend all.

Chapter 12

Everlasting Strength

O everlasting Strength; Uphold us in the way
Bring us, in spite of foes, at length,
To joy and light and day!

— Rev. L. R. West

Living in the shelter of God is everlasting strength.

From everlasting to everlasting you are God.[1]

Everlasting is an attribute of the character of God: absolute, perpetual, unchanging, boundless, unending, eternal.

It is everlasting.

Do you not know? Have you not heard? The Lord is the everlasting God, the creator of the ends of the earth. He will not grow tired or weary, and his understanding no one can fathom. He gives strength to the weary and increases the power of the weak.[2]

When we are joined to Him, His strength is appropriated to us as everlasting.

Review your life.

What has been lasting?

What has not?

What have you kept?

What have you lost?

I remember wishing that a doll had been saved from my childhood.

Gone.

I remember wishing that some newspaper clippings from some of my performances in plays had been saved.

Gone.

I remember wishing there was a family photograph of my parents with my sister Judy and me together.

Gone.

I remember wishing for video clips of early Navy life with Roy.

Gone.

The list can be endless.

How do we begin to ascertain what is significant?

A frame of reference is needed.

We all want something to hold on to that reflects our journey – something lasting.

As Roy and I embraced married life, in time our children were born. Then consciously I began to catalogue our life together in photographs, journals, letters, gifts, trips, special celebrations, graduations, our children's marriages and the birth of grand children…creating memory and, most of all, our story.

Loss inevitably comes and it did.

In burying parents one's childhood is also buried.

After the death of my father, I managed to find one photograph in his belongings of him and my beautiful young mother holding me as a baby.

Indeed it is a treasure, a documentation that I was…for there is no other.

I framed it for it is a visible image of my life as a child, one I could hold on to for they are both gone.

When I became the matriarch of the Norris/Hall women, I rededicated myself to my God privately and publicly at mother's funeral.

"…regularly rededicate yourself to God."[3]

Faded photographs, an antique bed, a gold ring, a family watch, a favorite jacket, a Bible present to us symbols of the rites of passage in our families.

Can we hold on to them?

Yes, for awhile.

What we discover through the power of story is what they held on to.

The unfolding of faith in an everlasting God is something to hold on to and they did.

So must we.

The family Bibles left behind revealed study, notes, a search for answers, a call to God for strength.

In the Great Depression years from 1929-1942, money was scarce. Stock markets crashed and banks failed. Jobs were gone. America entered World War II in late 1941. Women at home also worked in factories while men went off to fight on foreign soil. My mother talked about how they survived.

She said that when one looked around in those days no able-bodied men were left behind in America. There were only women and children. Ration books were distributed for sugar, coffee and other food items. Soups lines came as hard times fell, but a Mighty God sustained. Illness and death knocked on the doors of homes but faith in an everlasting God gave strength to hold on to. Uncertainty and fear stalked but they carried hopes and dreams for a future because they trusted in an everlasting God who held them in His hands.

He never lets go of His children.

He didn't then and He doesn't now.

My friend Rhonda knows all about a faith that holds on.

Singing next to her in choir is a complete delight. She is a tall African-American woman in stature with a warm, rich voice that rolls out seemingly effortlessly. She exudes the joy of the Lord. Her knowledge of music is exacting and her notes are always strong. She's a powerhouse. A ready smile and a friendly hug are always a ready welcome. One is energized by just singing next to her...strengthened.

Read her words as she writes her story for it is a window to her strength.

"Tears flowed like the storm surge in the levees of hurricane Katrina. The monsoon's torrential rainfall began for my husband Victor and me in May 2005 as we were confronted with the potential of best friends who might not grow old together. The sober seminal moment stealthily struck our lives like the deadly venom of a black mamba snake with lightning speed and without the specific antivenin. It is known to be 100% deadly. The blow delivered was 'Aggressive, Stage IV,

Metastatic breast cancer.' The door to the beauty of life began to close. Ironically and eerily foreboding, the head of this most deadly snake in the world is said to resemble a coffin.

Our medical trek began. Four years of tests and procedures encompassing different types of chemo accompanied a radical mastectomy along with radiation and drug therapies. The side effects were devastating and caused a plethora of never-ending debilitating changes: hair loss, nausea, eye problems, excessive and chronic fatigue, muscle pain, weight gain, cognitive disparities, breathing impairment, gastro-intestinal difficulty, declining balance, loss of sense of taste and more.... I found myself looking up into the heavens for help.... This place of despair was breathtaking, unimaginable, overwhelming, and yet the darkness was pierced with brilliant points of unfathomable light.... Our spiritual, soul and body continued to look up for the appreciation of *this* day in our journey...His Day. Would we align our choices with the distinct providence of His eye toward our future or would we choose our tunnel vision? His promises to us were unwavering, eternal, reliable, enduring, imperishable, unfailing, and indestructible because they were found in His unfaltering, immutable everlasting Word."

The Lord is my strength and my shield; my heart trusts in Him, and I am helped, therefore my heart greatly rejoices, and with my song I will praise Him. Psalm 28:7

After reading her words, I then understood the strength of her song.

She continued, "What happens when the questions regarding your cancer journey never stop and the temporal answers don't answer?"

The eternal God is your everlasting refuge, and underneath are the everlasting arms. Deuteronomy 33:27

"When all the information, remedies and evaluations meant to alleviate confusion and bring calm deliver instead oxymoronic prepackaged words that leave you baffled and in a daze," the Word of God strengthens.

The LORD is the strength of his people, a fortress of salvation for his anointed one. Psalm 28:3

She continued, "The answer is simple."

The fear of the Lord is the beginning of wisdom: all who follow his precepts have good understanding, to him belongs eternal praise. Psalm 111:10.

Rhonda planned to seek Him, follow Him and praise Him through all the twists and turns for His Word was a light for her path and a lamp unto her feet.

"My God is not filled with quaint platitudes and repetitive mantras…but He is a testament of provisional everlasting strength. His faithfulness is biblical and personal. His promises are ceaseless. His care is steadfast. He is the God of hope for tomorrow, despite your diagnosis."

For I know the plans I have for you,' declares the Lord, 'plans to prosper you and not to harm you, plans to give you hope and a future. Jeremiah 29:11

"He is the one who speaks softly to the recesses of your heart, 'I, not the doctors have numbered your days. I alone know your timeline.'"

Man's days are numbered; you have decreed the number of his months…. Job 14:5

God alone knows the bookends of our lives.

"He is the one who comforts and sustains after disfiguring surgery. What once was a svelte physique became a physically weaker frame, with an incongruous chest wall."

Praise be to the God of our Lord Jesus Christ, the Father of compassion and the God of all comfort, who comforts us in all our troubles.... II Corinthians 2:1:3-4

My comfort in suffering is this: your promise preserves my life. Psalm 119:30

She reminds us that His mantle of Love heals our expectation with fresh surrender.

"He gently weeps and gingerly carries you through the gale force of post chemical infusion pain."

The righteous cry out and the Lord hears them.... The Lord is close to the broken hearted and saves those who are crushed in spirit. A righteous man may have many troubles, but the Lord delivers him.... Psalm 34:17-19

She knows God hears the cries of His children and comes to deliver them through.

"Though the shock of the diagnosis stung like the bite of the poisonous black mamba, I am strengthened, comforted and encouraged continually by the sovereign One who knows the beginning and the end. It is not surprising that the predominant method for producing the antitoxin for dangerous snakes is done so by introducing trace amounts of venom into the blood of a lamb. In time, an immune response is generated producing antibodies which later can be harvested for the benefit of others. My Father provided His son Jesus Christ, the Lamb of God.

He entered this world as the only antidote for our illness, sin. His blood was given to inoculate our lives with the miracle of forgiveness. The Blood of the Lamb indeed is precious for it was the everlasting seal of pardon, the final harbinger needed to secure our shelter in the storm. He is the Healer Jehovah Rapha, the One who heals on both sides of eternity.

Hallelujah to the Lamb of Glory!

"Praise God for the everlasting shelter of the Blood of the Lamb who was and is and is to come!"

Strength comes to seekers who encounter the Christ of the Word.

The woman at the well received it through a cup of water as documented in John 4:10.

Her weakness, which morally compromised her life, was infused at last with the strength given in pardon through an everlasting God.

The woman who hemorrhaged for 12 years knew if she could but touch the hem of Christ's garment she would be healed. Her story is found in Mark 5:25-34.

Her weakened health was restored because of her faith in a God of everlasting strength.

Rhonda lived in the Word of God and uncovered day by day the strength needed to hold on to the One who proved His strength was everlasting.

He holds her still.

Christ came to wipe away our tears, carry our hurts, heal our bodies and equip us to believe that we will survive storms and even trample on snakes.

God's strength is everlasting from generation to generation.

Faith in Him is taught in the home, lived at work, taken to school, bred in leadership in the community, nurtured in churches and raised up in a nation.

Sacrifice and adversity are tenets tested by trial.

Life with God is everlasting.

The Bible is still with us.

Faith remains.

The praying fruitful lives of the godly can be reproduced as the everlasting strength of God continues to inspire and equip all who live in the shelter of faith.

Men and women before us pursued it and men and women after us will also if we will be faithful.

God has made everything beautiful in its time. He has also set eternity in the hearts of men; yet they cannot fathom what God has done from beginning to end. [4]

We need their stories.

They are a part of ours.

Mary Slessor, a Scottish missionary, seemed an unlikely candidate for a life to be poured out in the Calabar mission founded on the West coast of Africa. She was born in 1848 in Aberdeen, Scotland into a humble working class home. Mary was the second of seven children. Her mother's gentle faith was the example from which she first learned God's love. Her father, a shoemaker by trade, early on had fallen into intemperance and dark days descended for the family. Lack of resources to care for the family forced them to move into the industrial town of Dundee. There he became a laborer in one of the mills but his habit with the bottle continued. Wherever Mrs. Slessor lived she always found a church with a Sunday school for her children and they attended regularly. The church became the bright spot to look forward to as the week progressed. Mary heard about missionaries in faraway places like Calabar that served a God of love who called them to come. She tucked the thought away to ponder. Near her home lived a fiery little widow who spoke to Mary one day about faith in Christ and the arrows of truth pierced her heart. She believed, received and became a Christian. Dire financial straits at home forced Mrs. Slessor to find work in a textile factory. At age 11 little Mary joined her mother learning to weave under her tutelage for half days and attending school the other half days.

Mary advanced and began to earn more money. Her wages were desperately needed for the family. Long hours in the factory usurped time but she managed to read a book now and then by placing it on the loom and seizing time from sleep as well. These early years were filled with hardships as the father continued his downward spiral into alcohol addiction. He spent every penny on his consuming habit. Mary had to go to pawn shops to help add to the monies needed to bring sustenance to their meager lives. She and her mother prayed constantly just to hear his clumsy footsteps in the evening and they prayed that this secret would be contained within the family.

What strength it must have taken for them to overcome the obstacles they faced daily.

These beginnings marked her difficult life with reality but, "The reaction on her character deepened her sympathy and pity for others.... Suffering in the innocent has its compensations. It made her the fierce champion of little children, and the refuge of the weak and the oppressed. It prepared her also for the task of combating the trade in spirits on the West Coast of Africa, and for dealing with the drunken tribes amongst whom she came to dwell. Her experience was indeed the beginning of her training for the work she had to accomplish in the future." [5]

In the coming years, she grew in her love of God. "To think that behind all the strain and struggle of the world there was a Personality, not a thought or a dream...but One who was actual and close to her, over flowing with love and compassion and ready to listen to her, to heal, guide and strengthen her – was marvelous. She wished to know all He had to tell her in order that she might rule her conduct according to His Will.... Most of all it was the story of Jesus she pored over and thought about. His Divine majesty, the beauty and grace of His life, the pathos of His death on the cross affected her inexpressibly. She loved Him with a love so intense that she surrendered herself more and more. It was this passion of love and gratitude, this abandonment of self, this longing for service that carried her into her life's work." [6]

For 14 years, Mary Slessor, worked and carried the glow of Christ in her, giving His life away at the factory, in a downtown mission and to the children in the slums. Then at the age of 28, the opportunity to go to Calabar came and she was ready. In 1874 the news of David Livingstone's death stirred her nation and she bid farewell to Scotland leaving for the mission in Calabar.

Her life in West Africa consisted of hunger and thirst in a blazing African sun, tropical fevers, and drunken cannibals brandishing loaded muskets. She learned to master hundreds of frenzied natives and faced death a thousand times to bring the Redemption story of Jesus' love. Mary rescued unwanted babies cast off to die — especially twins, who were thought to bring a curse.

She countered superstition with the love of God. Once she nursed a chief's son whom she found after he had fallen out of tree. He became worse. Tribal doctors were then called in and he died. The chief wanted them all to die. *Ma* as Mary was known stood against him. He was furious and then threatened her. She bowed her head in prayer asking for strength and patience and after several days of battling this crisis. Mary won out for he recanted and let them live. How did this lone Scottish woman endure such an ordeal? "Had I not felt my Saviour close beside me, I would have lost all reason."

Empowered by that Divine Presence she held her ground and preached to the natives.

Quoting the words of Jesus, '*He that heareth my word and believeth on Him that sent me, hath everlasting life, and shall not come into condemnation; but is passed from death into life*', for she sought to show the terrors of divine judgment and the wonders of life everlasting.... "In Christ, we become new creatures. His life becomes ours. Take that word *life* and turn it over and over and press it and try to measure it, and see what it yields. Eternal life comprises everything we yearn for. Do not your hearts yearn for this?"[7]

She lived a life of rescue, mediation, sacrifice and prayer.

In her Bible these thoughts were penned:

"God is never behind time. A gracious woman has gracious friendships. We must see and know Christ before we can teach. No gift or genius or position can keep us safe or free from sin.

Good is good, but it is not enough; it must be God."[8]

Her life with God was marked by His everlasting strength.

In Calabar, West Africa, Mary Slessor's life is a testament of everlasting faith.

In another century, a continent was impacted because of the passion of one woman who pressed into the Life of Christ, persevering out of His love.

Will we?

Her story stretches ours.

Faith will be tested.

"God doesn't test us in order to find out something he doesn't already know. He tests us so we can learn about ourselves and His love, power and faithfulness."[9]

Overcoming overcomes.

Mary lived in the shelter of faith and she left it behind.

Faith in an everlasting God strengthens us.

Trust in the Lord forever for in the Lord Jehovah is everlasting strength.[10]

Her story continues.

So does ours.

Come to the Shelter.

Find strength to keep watch.

How great is your goodness which you have stored up for those who fear you, which you bestow in the sight of men on those who take refuge in you. In the shelter of your presence you hide them from the intrigues of men. [11]

A WATCHFUL EYE

1. Why do we struggle for significance?
2. How do powerful stories like Mary Slessor's strengthen us?
3. What will you leave behind that is lasting?

WATCHWORD

Jesus! Confirm my heart's desire
To work, and speak and think for Thee,
Still let me guard the holy fire,
And stir up Thy gift in me.

— Charles Wesley

PRAYER WATCH

Everlasting Father;

Humbled, we bow down.

Amazed at the sustaining power of your strength to generations past, we repent of shallow unproductive lives.

Awed at the gift of faith I given abundantly in overwhelming adversity, we cry "Abba, strengthen our resolve."

Altered by YOUR consuming love once more, we recommit our way unto YOU.

YOURS is righteous and lasting.

Forgive our contrived notions of self aggrandizement.

THEE, not me, Lord.

We cast them down.

We raise up the CROSS of Jesus.

Committed afresh we pledge to serve Our King wherever He leads.

Some of us will go to the ends of the earth and some will walk around the corner.

YOUR everlasting Life must be made visible in ours, recognizable and renewed moment to moment.

YOU have asked us to carry it somewhere to someone.

YOUR strength is everlasting, boundless and eternal.

In Jesus' Name, we shall.

CHAPTER 13

RISING STRENGTH

Faith is kept alive in us and gathers strength, more from practice than speculation.

— Joseph Addison

Living in the shelter of God is a rising strength.

Life with God begins in Jesus.

It still does.

Scripture pronounces His birth, death and resurrection.

His life among men was a life of prayer.

In John 17 we read of Jesus' prayer to His Father for believers present and those to come.

It is a prayer for us.

Hear the tender and impassioned heart of love;

I have revealed you to those whom you gave me out of the world.

They were yours; you gave them to me and they have obeyed your word.

Now they know everything you have given me comes from you.

For I gave them the words you gave me and they accepted them.

They knew with certainty that I came from you, and they believed that you sent me.

I pray for them.

I am not praying for the world, but for those you have given me, for they are yours.

All I have is yours, and all you have is mine.

And glory has come to me through them.

I will remain in the world no longer, but they are still in the world, and I am coming to you.

Holy Father, protect them by the power of your name — the name you gave me so they may be one as we are one....

Sanctify them by your truth; your word is truth.... My prayer is not for them alone. I pray also for all of those who will believe in me through their message, that all of them may be one....[1]

With this prayer on our behalf, we embrace once again the rich depository of life in Christ Jesus. We are strengthened by His longing for our protection. As we ponder His words of unity, *that all may be one*, there is a call rising,

A call to live in truth,

A call to be set apart to do so,

A call to be a people of the Word, to be the body of Christ.

He is the head.

Instead we will speak the truth in love, growing in every way more and more like Christ, who is the head of his body, the church. He makes the whole body fit together perfectly. As each part does its own special work, it helps the other parts grow, so that the whole body is healthy and growing and full of love.[2]

So it is with Christ's body, we are many parts of one body, and we all belong to each other.[3]

He calls a people out of the nations of the world to be one people.

What do we look like?

Everyone.

His Life in us is identified in others.

Our cultures may be different, our songs of worship, our language, our dress, our customs, our ways of communication but if we are His we will know each other as family.

Jesus Christ is the centerpiece of the Christian Faith, the common denominator, the pole star.

The Gospel has been, is and will forever be, the Good News of Jesus Christ.

Men and women have lived and died for it, because they upheld it and believed it.

Sixteenth century reformer and scholar William Tyndale who translated the Bible into the early modern English of his day was burned at the stake for so doing. His final words were "Lord, open the King of England's eyes."

God heard and today we have the Bible.

Chinese missionary Watchman Nee became a Christian at age 17 and committed himself to spreading the Gospel to his native China. In 1952 he was imprisoned for his faith. Approximately 400 churches have been raised up in China through his life in ministry. He was in prison until he died in 1972. In his final letter written on the day he died he wrote, "In my sickness, I still remain joyful at heart." [4]

Joyful and faithful to the end, his life continues to inspire thousands to follow Christ, to rise up.

Wherever two or three are gathered together as my followers, I am there among them. [5]

Our God is among us when we become one in Him.

We are called to be His body.

Speaking the truth in love, we will in all things grow up unto Him who is the Head, that is, Christ. From Him the whole body, joined together by every supporting ligament, grows and builds itself up in love, as each part does its work.[6]

A physical body has feet and hands, ears and eyes, a brain and a mouth. Inside the body a beating heart operates in concert with expansive lungs working around the clock together with all the other organs to establish health.

The body functions as an entity.

Across the world today, cultures are fractured because of Godlessness.

A look at our nation verifies this disturbing observation.

America is being shaken and we are witnessing the crumbling of our walls.

Economically, we now live in a world of credit and instant gratification.

The fallacy of this choice is destroying our security.

Spiritually, our lifestyles are eliminating any God consciousness.

Our discontent is driving our hearts to move away from the goodness of God, the source of contentment.

Our greed for more has brought us less, for only He is the true Provider.

Our rebellion, which has led us from a God-ordained way of life to a government-orchestrated way of life, is a substitution which preempts Him.

In short, we are systematically deleting God from our way of life,

And it shows.

Once we had longing for Him.

As a deer longs for flowing streams, so my soul longs for you, Lord.
My soul thirsts for God, for the living God....[7]

We were created for intimacy and fellowship with Him.

He longs for us.

But now we have reneged, subtly slipping away at first until the holy urgings to which we once responded have been nullified, stilled.

In Mark Buchanan's book, *Things Unseen,* we read a scathing indictment of our condition. "We have become so self-indulgent that we devour ourselves.... In fact, self pity and self indulgence, boredom and despair, envy, greed – such (represent) yearning gone sour. They are just the greasy residue that remains after yearning has gone unfulfilled too many times. A sadness-like ash settles on our doings and our desires. We find trinkets to fiddle with, trivia to distract us. A once burning zeal dwindles to a dry itch, and everything becomes a frantic attempt to get the passion back, or a plodding resignation to its death." [8]

Our spiritual depravity has left us weak, depleted with a loss of virtue.

But God is still with us.

He has not deleted us.

Life with God is filled with His goodness and it fortifies us with a rising strength.

We need to come home.

We can begin again.

He is calling us.

We have created impossibilities that sink promise and suffocate faith.

In the book of Ezekiel we read of a striking miraculous account of a valley of dry bones.

"The prophet Ezekiel was a captive along with the rest of the nation of Israel. The nation of Israel had fallen away from God. God had withdrawn His protection and blessing. This resulted in Israel being conquered by their enemies.... The nation had died spiritually when they had forsaken God and then died physically when they were taken to serve in a foreign land." [9]

Captive now and broken, all hope had seemingly vanished.

Ezekiel was saddened and despondent.

The truth concerning the state of the nation was staggering.

God knew his anguish and intervened in an unusual way. He took him to another place in a vision.

Ezekiel wrote, *The Hand of the Lord was upon him...and by the Spirit of God, he was set down in the middle of the valley; it was full of bones...and behold there were many on the surface of the valley; and lo, they were very dry. And He said to me 'Son of man, can these bones live?' And I answered, 'O Lord God, Thou knowest.'* [10]

There were many bones and they were very dry.

Then God spoke and said, *'Ezekiel, speak...to these bones and say, Dry bones listen to the word of the Lord'*! [11]

And he did.

The Sovereign Lord says, 'I will put flesh and muscles on you and cover you with skin. I will put breath in you, and you will come to life. Then you will know that I am the Lord.' [12]

A distinct noise was heard, then the sounds of rattling bones coming together but there was more. Sinew and skin were forming perfectly around individual skeletal frames – a body was being put together inside out,

But there was no breath.

Without breath there is no life.

Once again God spoke and said, *'Ezekiel speak…to the winds… and say, this is what the Sovereign Lord says, Come O breath from the four winds. Breathe into these bodies so they may live again.'* [13]

Ezekiel did as he was told and breath came into these bodies and they stood up as a vast army.

Jesus spoke in parables, stories within a story.

We can visualize truth in stories.

He speaks of word pictures and visions so we can learn the magnitude of His power.

This account moves on and the army comprised of the houses of Israel and Judah was brought together as one people. God makes a covenant of peace with them and said, *'I will make my home among them; I will be their God and they will be my people'.* [14]

Their disobedience had led them astray as a nation.

So has ours.

A gasping faith must return to the God of scripture.

Are we a valley of dry bones that has no life?

Have we run out of resources?

Is the future a dead end?

No, our God is not dead.

And He is on His Watch yearning for us to hear His call.

What was wasted can be brought back to life…through Him.

God did not personally address many people in the Bible, but He chose to speak to Ezekiel.

Incredulous as the request must have seemed, Ezekiel heard and obeyed God.

Obedience is pledging to do the next thing, taking the next step.

It is following through.

Our God pursues us.

Do we pursue Him?

"God is in a relentless pursuit of a people who will be gathered from the ends of the earth to join together…forming a community of love that is more powerful and glorious than all the kingdoms of the world." [15]

The Love of God retrieves a people from despair and turns them toward devotion.

F. B. Meyer, English pastor, author, teacher understood the compelling call of God's Love.

Born in 1847 his distinguished educational background prepared him through scholarship to be a man of great influence. He was a devoted student of God's Word all his life.

"With his gifts he might have risen to eminence in any sphere…but with a big heart and a wide sympathy he remained true to his convictions until the end. He was great because he confessed that he was little, and brave because he knew that any man could be a coward." [16]

His life's motto, "Make the most of me that will make the most for Thy glory," reflects a desire to please God and follow hard after Him.

The author of over 40 books, he pastored for 15 years in England and did mission work in South Africa and the Far East.

He wore himself out decrying the social ills which choke morality from a society. Morality builds character, redeems virtue and revives a nation. It still does. Even beauty emerges again.

The perception of beauty is a moral test.

— Henry David Thoreau

"During his long and fruitful life, he preached more than 16,000 sermons. An author said, 'The phrasing of Meyer's sermons was simple and direct; he polished his discourses as an artist polished a perfect stone. There was always glowing imagery in his words; his speech was pastoral, lovely as an English valley washed in sunlight.... In his day, great wars raged. Those who went to hear him forgot the battles'." [17]

A man whose words wooed others wooed them to follow God.

His Life with God was steadfast.

"Deep Fellowship with Christ is impossible unless you set yourself to its cultivation – Friendship cannot be made by glimpses.... Perhaps in all the universe none can satisfy God's yearning heart as man can. We are made in His likeness. God seeketh such." [18]

God's yearning for us creates a yearning for Him, but we want to be safe.

In the book, *The Lion, the Witch and the Wardrobe,* C. S. Lewis developed intriguing characters drawn from his imagination cast dramatically through the power of story.

He wrote this series between 1949 and 1954.

Narnia is a fictionalized place where animals talk and some even have mythological bodies. Fantasy and mystery merge in adventure but the real crux of the story is a moral one.

It is the battle between good and evil.

This battle continues.

The Beaver family begins to discuss Aslan the Lion with Lucy and Susan.

"You'll understand when you see him."

"But shall we see him?" asked Susan.

"That's what I brought you here for. I'm to lead you where you shall meet him," said Mr. Beaver.

"Is – is he a man?" asked Lucy.

"Aslan, a man!" said Mr. Beaver sternly. "Certainly not. I tell you he is a King of the wood and the son of the great Emperor-beyond-the-Sea. Don't you know who the King of Beasts is? Aslan is a lion – *the* lion, the great lion."

"Ooh!" said Susan, "I thought he was a man. Is he – quite safe? I shall feel rather nervous about meeting a lion."

"That you will, dearie, and make no mistake," said Mrs. Beaver; "if there's anyone who can appear before Aslan without their knees knocking, they are either braver than most or else just silly."

"Then he isn't safe?" said Lucy.

"Safe?" said Mr. Beaver; "don't you hear what Mrs. Beaver tells you? Who said anything about safe? Course he isn't safe. But he's good. He's the King I tell you." [18]

Farther along Lewis writes, "People who have not been in Narnia sometimes think that a thing cannot be good and terrible at the same time?" [19]

Can it?

When the movie by the same name was released in America, people flocked to it not knowing what to expect.

I wept and rejoiced the first time I saw it.

Yes, I did both at the same time, interspersed, continuously, with joy and pathos.

I experienced sadness over the plight of evil as it assaults the minds of men and joy over the victory of the warrior King who champions justice and wins.

I was filled with the sense of the glorious goodness of a God who would guide a man to create such an intrigue over fifty years ago. Indeed it was a parable of good and evil. Then in the gracious timing of God it exploded onto the cinema screen in 2005 bringing its impact to life visually for the peoples of the world living in the technological age of movies, computers, iPods, cell phones and media of every sort.

It caused my faith to rise up and surge in a mighty wave of longing to follow my God and King who always means good for us in spite all that threatens.

Yes, we want to be safe.

It is a natural desire and a prayer that we pray daily for ourselves and others,

But we are called to seek first the Kingdom of God.

Seek first the Kingdom of God and his righteousness and all these things shall be added unto you.[20]

When we seek to follow Him, there will be risk and perhaps loss, but He is training us to trust in His goodness for it always prevails.

In Narnia, the goodness of the Beaver family that was extended to Lucy resulted in their losing their home even though they led her to Aslan.

Mr. Tumnus, the Faun, lost his home and was turned into a statue for aiding Lucy.

Danger and goodness do exist together.

The stories of the Bible are filled with tales of triumph and retribution where suffering opened the way to establish the goodness of God.

In the struggle of our nation for freedom, lives are lost, people are displaced, property is seized or destroyed and yet we came through because we believe in the cause of freedom.

Righteousness is a way of life based on doing the right thing for the right reason.

There will always be a cost.

Jesus wasn't safe either but He was and is good.

The leaders of His day were filled with a lust for power, insatiable greed and frantic fear.

They targeted His goodness.

He gave His life on a Cross for a wicked and perverse world.

An evil, mocking moment of cruelty that brought death and burial to Him was presumed by many to end His life but three days later, heavenly light flooded an empty Tomb.

The ugliness of sin was exchanged for the beauty of His goodness and the Risen Christ called forth an army of followers which revolutionized the world then and we are rising once again.

He is calling us to stand up and move our nation back to Him but we must be moved first.

In Him there will be a rising strength.

He is ultimately safe for believing in Him provides a safe passage to a place called Glory.

In Martin Luther's words, a hymn of reformation is rising in our hearts, resounding in our souls calling us:

A mighty Fortress is our God, a bulwark never failing;

Our helper, He, amid the flood of mortal ills prevailing:

For still our ancient foe doth seek to work us woe;

His craft and power are great, and, armed with cruel hate.

On earth is not his equal.

Did we in our own strength confide, our striving would be losing;

Were not the right Man on our side, the Man of God's own choosing:

Dost ask who that may be? Christ Jesus, it is He;

Lord Saboath, His Name, from age to age the same,

And He must win the battle.

And though this world with devils filled, should threaten to undo us,

We will not fear, for God hath willed His truth to triumph through us.

Do you hear the call?

Rise up and follow Him.

The Lord reigns.... He is armed with strength. (21)

Find the strength to keep watch.

Live in the shelter.

How great is your goodness, which you have stored up for those who fear you, which you bestow in the sight of men on those who take refuge in you. In the shelter of your presence you hide them from the intrigues of men. (22)

A Watchful Eye

1. Do you know that God yearns for you?

2. Are you willing to take your place in His army?

3. Will His Goodness carry you through?

Watchword

You cannot run away from weakness; you must sometimes fight it out or perish; And if that be so, why not now, and where you stand?

— Robert Louis Stevenson

Prayer Watch

Mighty Father;

Long ago YOU knew we would need strength to fight the battles ahead.

We are fledglings in our faith.

We lean more than we lead.

We look more than we long.

We discount our small victories as trivial without gratitude and languish by losing sight of YOU.

Weakened and impotent we fall away from our calling and begin to fade into the culture taking on its nebulous mediocrity, blending easily into obscurity.

Apathy replaces discontentment which replaces self absorption and then we abdicate our godly allegiance.

We politely but quietly slip away from YOU.

The descent is swift but not absolute.

For somewhere in the distance, a hymn, a scripture, a story, a book, a prayer jars our souls and our yearning for YOU begins to rise up once more within us.

YOU ARE STILL ON WATCH.

YOU ARE CALLING YOUR PEOPLE.

YOU ARE WAITING FOR US.

Oh Father, we come and bow down in remorse for our negligence, our rebellion.

Forgive our sin.

We turn back to YOU.

We stand up and declare that we will follow YOU.

The valley of dry bones is now an army breathing in vitality through YOUR GOODNESS.

Our faith has been resuscitated.

YOUR strength is rising and so are we.

In deepest love we enter the arena of Truth armed with hope once again.

CHAPTER 14

LIVING IN THE SHELTER OF HIS PRESENCE

Forever is composed of nows
— Emily Dickenson

Living in the shelter of His presence is strength forever.

This is Life with God.

I am God Almighty; Live in my Presence and be devout.[1]

Being present to God begins with surrender.

I am Almighty God; Walk before Me and be blameless.[2]

He summons us.

Presence involves relationship.

Relationship takes time to build.

He is always present but are we?

Turning our minds toward God is a choice.

"The sense of God being with us is His gift, on one condition: that we try to be with Him."[3]

We all learn in different ways but we can all learn if we seek Him.

How did God teach me this process?

I look back at my husband's Navy career which spanned 30 years.

I wrote hundreds of letters.

He was away from home on Navy deployments for almost 14 years, cumulatively.

In romance, if we have a beloved that is thousands of miles away, we must choose to think upon them for they are absent. As we position our thoughts upon them they become real to us and our love grows.

This is what I did.

Staying connected was important.

We were a team and purposed to increase the span of our relationship by deliberate remembrance, gifts, phone calls, photographs and a covenant of prayer.

Roy would go to sea on ships and lead men.

I would stay at home and raise children.

We both had to be responsible.

My goal was to keep our marriage alive and to raise children to honor God, honor their father and contribute.

I longed to become a woman of prayer.

I asked God to lead me.

I prayed.

I practiced.

Prayer is loving God back.

It was the catalyst of growing my relationship with Him.

At first it was just a step toward God, and then the act became a desire to express love and receive it. Finally it evolved into a precious abiding privilege.

Every time I moved toward Him, He was there.

Cultivate a pure and upright intention toward God

— Francis de Fenelon

How did this reality finally manifest?

The loneliness of my husband's absences brought me into a spacious place where my void merged into a conscious seeking after God's presence.

But you have set my feet in a spacious place. [4]

I remember feeling a stirring within me to worship and praise my God. I needed to keep short accounts of my personal wrongs through confession of sin. I wanted to grow close to Him. I had challenges daily which required decisions. My faith needed spiritual oxygen. I wanted to learn to pray for others. Prayer became my first line of offense and my last line of defense.

"Prayer does not blind us to the world, but it transforms our vision of the world, and makes us see it, all people and all history of humankind, in the light of God." [5]

It set up God cognizance for me daily as my awareness was honed by compassion and compelled to act.

But then simultaneously I developed a hunger for the study of the Word of God. In it His character is revealed. The more I learned about Him the more I learned about me. My love for His Word flourished.

I found I could live in it for it was a book of instruction, comfort, mercy, compassion, justice, grace, forgiveness, hope and most of all Love.

I discovered His presence in His Word.

He speaks to us through it.

I listened and heard.

The Bible was a love letter to me and I embraced it.

Change came.

Faith routed fear.

Assurance brought acceptance.

Peace replaced self pity.

"Most loneliness is pain...peering into mirrors of self pity with hope of seeing someone else to blame it on."[6]

I let go and let God carry me.

I found my way home.

As I learned to pray and as I studied His word, His presence became ever present to me, a comfort.

It is He who creates this shelter within us if we are present to Him.

I have set the Lord always before me. Because he is at my right hand I shall not be moved.[7]

Life interrupts.

He stabilizes.

Roy and I both needed to live from a center found in Christ alone.

This was our training ground for survival.

It worked.

When Roy would return home from long months at sea, we would celebrate and in gratitude thank God for bringing us through once more. This unusual and erratic lifestyle birthed the pattern of living in the shelter of His presence.

I can now reflect upon those years as blessing and preparation.

My writing finds its foundation in the spiritual disciplines of prayer and Bible study that I learned in those years while searching for a devotional relationship with God.

My love for encouraging others is a byproduct of giving back in thanksgiving to others for all He gave to me.

My passion to pray for others was birthed from the reality that prayer matters to Him and therefore to me.

Life with God strengthens us to bring His life to all we encounter.

How great is your goodness which you have stored up for those who fear you, which you bestow in the sight of men on those who take refuge in you. In the shelter of your presence you hide them from the intrigues of men.[8]

God has a storehouse of goodness, favor and blessing to give to all who follow Him. It becomes our refuge, a place where we are hidden in Him, strengthened and equipped to go back into the world to be a conduit of His life.

Dwelling in the shelter of His presence, we receive God cognizance.

How does it unfold?

He calls us to faith and then summons us to keep watch.

I have posted watchmen on your walls, O Jerusalem; they will never be silent day and night.[9]

We are to be watchmen on the walls.

The eyes of the Lord are in every place, keeping watch over the evil and the good.[10]

He is on watch as well.

We are weak.

He is strong.

A watch is a call to act.

Beauty is a watch.

Confucius wisely reminds us, "Everything has beauty but not everyone sees it."

Keeping watch over beauty will bring us to delights of nature, art, literature and joy in Him for He creates beauty.

Johann von Goethe tells us that, "The soul that sees beauty may sometimes walk alone."

Our attempts to define our personal concept of beauty are one of either restraint or excess. One refines, the other exaggerates.

A spiritual focus on God will teach us how to achieve balance.

Beauty is balance.

Health is a watch.

French Aviator and writer, Antoine de Saint Exupery tells us, "It is only with the heart that one can see rightly; what is essential is invisible to the eye."

Keeping watch over health involves choice and instruction. Our minds and hearts must pursue knowledge and action. Caring for our physical bodies requires both.

Author Nathanael Hawthorne surmises, "A bodily disease which we look upon as whole and entire within itself may, after all, be but a symptom of some ailment in the spiritual part."

Seeking God affects our spiritual health. Neglecting Him breaks us.

Legacy is a Watch.

Seventeenth Century poet John Donne suggests, "Reason is our soul's left hand, faith be the right."

We will need both reason and faith to establish godliness for the generations that follow us.

Holding on to God is a legacy that will reproduce somewhere along the way.

Classical Roman poet, Virgil, living from 70 BC-19 BC wrote, "Your descendents shall gather your fruits."

To bear fruit, we must diligently seed faith.

Liberty is a watch.

James Madison reminds us of the power of conscience, "Conscience is the most sacred property of all."

Our God wants us to be aware and vigilant as a people, a conscience in our homes and in our nation.

When a seared conscience neutralizes truth, a nation falls.

Thomas Jefferson questions, "Can the liberties of a nation be sure when we remove their only firm basis, a conviction in the minds of the people, that these liberties are a gift from God?"

Our religious liberty is integral to the heart of America.

We must follow Him to perpetuate the standard of Biblical righteousness.

Every voice is important and so is ours.

God is the strength of my heart and my portion forever...as for me it is good to be near God, I have made the Sovereign Lord my refuge; I will tell of your deeds.[11]

Living in His presence provides strength forever.

What does it look like?

His Strength is **S**acramental...it integrates faith by connecting the dots in our lives.

His Strength is **H**oly...it presents a mind and heart set apart.

His Strength is **E**ncompassed…it is a body of friendship ever expanding faith.

His Strength is **L**uminous…it is a shining resiliency that reflects love.

His Strength is **T**ranscendent…it is a familial bond that unites.

His Strength is **E**verlasting…it is an eternal reality that is boundless.

His Strength is **R**ising…it is a prevailing hope energizing faith.

In Ben Sherwood's book, *The Survivors Club*, he documents the accounts of men and women who have survived crises of every imagination; mountain lion attacks; POW camps, airplane crashes, sea rescues, natural disasters and more. As he studied their survival mechanisms he identifies five categories: the fighter, the believer, the connector, the thinker and the realist. He submits that we probably share many of the characteristics indicative of all of these. However, he concludes that one is more predominant in us. In describing the believer's instinct for survival he says, "Faith is the most powerful universal survival tool. Your faith means you trust that God has a plan…and will steer you through difficult times…because God loves you…. In a crisis, faith gives you remarkable power and confidence to prevail. Then he quotes Dr. Harold Koenig of Duke University Medical Center who is one of the pioneers in the field of faith and health. 'This is a God who listens to prayer, who responds, who desires good for humanity.' You are never alone. Faith is your greatest comfort and mightiest weapon." [12]

Indeed it is.

Strength to persevere is promised to the faithful.

In the Word of God there is a moving story of power in weakness captured in the account of Gideon found in the book of Judges Chapters 6-7.

Israel as a nation had been disobedient to God for seven years so He gave them over into the hands of the Midianites. They in turn destroyed the crops and cattle and the children of Israel cried out to God for deliverance.

Hear what the Lord says to them: '*I brought you up out of Egypt; out of the land of slavery I snatched you from the power of Egypt and from the hand of all your oppressors. I drove them from before you, and gave them your land. I am the Lord your God; do not worship the gods of the Amorites, in whose land you live. But you have not listened to me.*' [13]

Disobedience begets consequence, but God heard their cries.

He was going to summon Gideon.

When the angel of the Lord appeared to Gideon, he said, 'The Lord is with you mighty warrior.' [14]

Gideon knew the calamity that surrounded all of them. He wondered why it had happened if indeed God was with them. Even the wonders that their fathers had so often acknowledged had not been evidenced.

Further instructions were given.

Go in the strength you have and save Israel out of Midian's hand. Am I not sending you?' [15]

Gideon protested, '*How can I save Israel? My clan is the weakest in Manasseh, and I the least in my family.*' [16]

The Lord answered, *'I will be with you when you strike down all the Midianites together.'* [17]

Gideon bargained with God further, preparing an offering, seeking more promises and in everything Gideon asked, God provided.

When the battle preparations were in place against the Midianites, Gideon had assembled 32,000 men.

The Lord confirmed that there were too many men. He was making sure *"that Israel may not boast against me that her own strength has saved her."* [18]

Therefore He established a way out by announcing that anyone who trembled with fear could turn back.

And 22,000 did.

Still the Lord declared there were too many men.

The last elimination evolved. The remaining men were taken down to the water. They were told to drink. There they were observed. Some would lap the water with their tongues like a dog and some would kneel down to drink.

Those who kneeled down would be dismissed for they could not drink and keep watch at the same time.

Only 300 used their hands to cup the water to their mouths. The rest kneeled down.

Gideon now had 300 men.

The odds were stacked against success.

God's odds are always weighty, worthy and winning.

During the night Gideon slipped down to the enemy's camp and overheard a conversation about a dream. When he heard the interpretation, he knew God would deliver him and his men into the victory promised.

Coming back to his men, Gideon worshipped God. Next he divided his men into three teams giving each a trumpet and an empty jar with torches inside. They were admonished to follow him, to watch him and do exactly as he did.

When the signal came to blow the trumpets and shout, "For the Lord and for Gideon", they did so.

At one point the jars were smashed and the men held up torches and blew their trumpets, shouting, "A sword for the Lord and for Gideon." The Midianites fled in fear for when 300 trumpets were blown, they turned on each other with swords and were crushed.

God was with Gideon.

Small becomes mighty when surrendered to God.

Scripture affirms the Lord's way…*my power is made perfect in weakness.* [19]

In our weakness, His strength becomes our provision.

Strength forever is enough strength.

Will we hear the Word of the Lord and follow Him?

Will we love His presence and live in fervency to Him?

Will we be counted in the 300 with Gideon who could drink and keep watch at the same time because God is with us?

Life with God is a community of Christ followers who live in the shelter of His presence and therefore become a presence for good outside it.

Life with God is transforming for it is born in His love.

What would this community of Christ followers look like?

"The efforts of God are culminating in the gathering of an obedient, disciplined freely gathered people who know in our day the life and powers of the kingdom of God. This community is a people of cross and crown, of courageous action and sacrificial love." [20]

In a world of self worship, they will rise to worship the King of Kings.

In a world of oppression, they will rise with imagination and faith for, "When God touches our imaginations, things of beauty emerge that can inspire us to leave this world a better place than we found it." [21]

In a world of broken promises, they will rise and take their watch for God is with them.

In 1940 when the world was in turmoil, Fred Tripp of Beloit, Wisconsin looked out of his hospital window at McCleary Hospital in Excelsior Springs, Missouri. He was inspired by an American flag flying atop the post office. This 70-year-old man had never had a painting lesson in his life but he decided to paint the American flag. A spirit of patriotism was sweeping the country and carried him along as he produced a compelling canvas, an artistic expression of what he felt about the Flag of his country. It was a six foot oil painting on canvas of a flag in repose. Lithographic reproductions reached the 200,000 mark when World War II broke out.

Roy and I discovered one of these framed prints in an antique mall last year and purchased it to celebrate our 45th wedding anniversary, which is the Fourth of July. It reminds us once more that we must commit our way day by day to our God, walking in His truth, loving others and being a people of faith who will never turn back.

The American flag symbolically represents our journey of freedom, a sentinel on watch over our land.

Here are the words written about the 1940 flag in repose:

"Softly draped with folds unstirred by even so much as a breath of summer breeze, Old Glory, our Flag…rests, waiting. It symbolizes the soul of America, standing in silent prayer before the Father of Light, receiving His guidance and protection through another perilous journey. It is the morning prayer of the American people, the prayer that arms them to the problems of the day with courage and cheer. Before it, America stands in reverence, realizing her sacred duty to mankind and her glorious destiny." [22]

God is calling us.

We shall live in His provisions of grace and mercy in gratitude.

"Gratitude generates optimism." [23]

Our Hope lies in Him.

In America we must keep watch over our nation.

Every generation has contributed to our liberty.

Our Faith in God is grounded by His Word.

Our relationship is nurtured through prayer.

Our service to one another is the overflow of His goodness.

His love in us is the love of Christ lived out unto others.

To do so we must have His strength.

Nehemiah had it.

Gideon received it,

And so shall we.

Living in the Shelter of His presence is living.

A hymn written in 1888 trumpets our journey with joy and hope:
Lead on Oh King Eternal,

We follow, not with fear,
For gladness breaks like morning
Where'er Thy face appears.
Thy cross is lifted over us,
We journey in its light;
The crown awaits the conquest;
Lead on, O God of might.

Sheltered in Him again and again as our forefathers were, we will continue to rise in love and triumph.

Deep to Deep, O Lord, crieth me.
Gathering strength I come, Lord, unto Thee.
Jesus of Calvary, smitten for me,
Ask what thou wilt but give love to me.

— Amy Carmichael

Hear His call.

Follow Him.

Keep watch.

Find strength.

Live in The Shelter.

THE SHELTER

Sovereign Father;
I come to YOU again.
This hidden place of refuge YOU have created within me is home.
I yearn to enter for YOU are present to guide me.
YOUR Word opens windows of assurance and YOUR light breaks through.
When I call to YOU in prayer, YOUR mantle of grace descends and I am comforted,
But there is more...my weakness, helplessness is exchanged for a rising strength that bonds YOUR Life to mine.

Christ in me rises.

Hope takes wings.

Faith reproduces.

YOUR goodness fills my heart with enough to share with another.

I emerge strengthened and equipped to take my watch.

YOUR people hear YOUR VOICE.

Our faith journey on this earth leads us to paths of Glory.

We're marching to Zion, beautiful, beautiful Zion.

We're marching upward to Zion, that beautiful City of God.

Increase our faith.

Bring the spring rain of new beginnings and the autumn rain of harvest to replenish our souls.

Let our lives become a prayer surge for others.

Be our pillow of rest on the highway.

Draw us to the Shelter of your Presence daily.

We kneel in weakness and rise in strength in Jesus' Name

Resolution One: I will live for God.

Resolution Two: If no one does, I still will.

— Jonathan Edwards

Sound the trumpet!

Join me.

Our God Reigns.

Billie Cash

Summer 2009

Collierville, TN

ABOUT THE AUTHOR

Billie Cash is an international retreat and conference speaker/ soloist. She has authored five other books, *Windows of Assurance, Light Breaking Through, Autumn Rain, PRAYERSURGE* and *A Pillow on the Highway*. With humor and insight, she brings accountability. A fresh authenticity and personal application are keys to her ministry.

Billie Cash
278 Colbert St. W.
Collierville, TN. 38017
Website: www.billiecash.com
E-mail: brcash@comcast.net
I'd love to hear from you!

NOTES

CHAPTER 1

1. Psalm 33:13-15, 16a,18-19

2. Psalm 32:19-20

3. Psalm 84:7

CHAPTER 2

1. 2 Corinthians 12:10

2. *Foster*: Richard Foster, *Life With God*, (San Francisco: Harper One, 2008), 72.

3. 2 Corinthians 12:7-12

4. Acts 9:4

5. Acts 9:5

6. Ibid.

7. Biblegateway.com −Commentaries, Chapter 9 , Paul's Conversion

8. *Gage*: Joy P. Gage, *The Treasures We Leave Behind*, (Colorado Springs: Cook Communications, 31-322001), 31.

9. Psalm 68:28

10. 2 Timothy 3: 10,11a,12

11. 2 Timothy 4:17a

12. Isaiah 21:6 AMP

13. Nehemiah 1:3

14. Nehemiah 1:5-6

15. Nehemiah 1:10

16. Nehemiah 2:8c

17. Nehemiah 2:17,20a

18. Nehemiah 4:9

19. Nehemiah 4:13-14

20. Nehemiah 4:20

21. Nehemiah 6:9c

22. Nehemiah 6:16

23. Proverbs 11:25

24. *Guinness*: Os Guinness, *The Call*, (Nashville: W Publishing group, 2003), 64-65.

CHAPTER 3

1. Psalm 96:6b

2. Psalm 74:17

3. Ecclesiastes 1:5-7

4. *Nouwen*: Henri Nowen, *The Return of The Prodigal*, (New York: Doubleday, 1994), 5.

5. Ibid., 94.

6. Luke 15:11

7. Luke 15:22

8. Luke 15:28-32

9. *Nouwen*: Henri Nouwen, *The Return of The Prodigal*, (New York: Doubleday, 1994), 15.

10. Psalm 96:6

11. http://www.cosmeticsurgerystatistics.com/statistics.html#2007-NEWS

12. I Peter 3:3-4

13. Psalm 27:4

14. Colossians 2:5b

15. Proverbs 31:17

CHAPTER 4

1. http://encarta.msn.com/text_761578429__0/Blood.html

2. www.customessaymeister.com/customessays/Nutrition/6925.htm

3. www.nutritionexplorations.org/parents/pyramid-keepinmind.asp

4. www.chetday.com/howmuchexercise.htm

5. Proverbs 23:7 KJV

6. Psalm 139:23,24

7. Acts 15:9b

8. I Samuel16:7b

9. Jeremiah 17:9

10. *Cash*: Billie Cash, *PRAYERSURGE*, (Greenville: Ambassador, 2005), 34.

11. Psalm 62:8

12. Hebrews 10:16

13. Deuteronomy 11:18

14. www.catholic.org

    article written by Deacon Keith Fournier7/12/2008

15. www.christianitytoday.com/ct/2007/july/25.30.html?start=3 " Cancer's Unexpected Blessings" by Tony Snow

16. *Hillman*: Os Hillman, *The Upside of Adversity*, (Ventura: Regal, 2006), 106.

17. James 1:12

18. http://kenny.netvios.com/pilot_saves_inaugeration.asp

19. www.azcentral.com/news/articles/2009/01/16/2009116 planereconstruct0116.html

20. http://spectator.org/blog/2009/01/16/no-athiests-on-flight-1549

21. Ephesians 1:17-18

22. *Foster*: Richard Foster, *Life With God*, (San Francisco: Harper One, 2008), 67.

CHAPTER 5

1. Psalm 145:4

2. *Cash*: Billie Cash, *Windows of Assurance*, (Greenville: Ambassador, 2001), 147.

3. Proverbs 27:23

4. 2 Corinthians 5:7

5. 1 John 1:7

6. Baczynska: Gabriella Baczynska; JonBoyle (2008-05-12). "Sendler: Savior of Warsaw Ghetto Children dies." *Washington Post* (The Washington Post Company), http://www.washingtonpost.com/wp-dyn/content/article/2008/05/12/AR2008051200522.html. Retrieved 2008-05-12

7. http://ap.google.com/article/ALeqM5jb2-
   kVEZARAOQGiSVSmc3dOK59NgD9OKE8TO2
   Retrieved 2008-05-13. "Polish Holocaust Hero Dies
   at age 98."

8. http://www.irenasendler.org/team.asp

9. http://en.wikipedia.org/wiki/Irena_Sendler

10. Ibid., 4.

11. http://www.telegraph.co.uk/news/1948680/
    %27Female-Schindler%27--Irene-Sendler,-who-saved-
    thousands-of-Jewish-children,-dies.html
    "Female Schindler", Irene Sendler, who saved Thousands
    of Jewish children, dies-Telegraph

12. http://www.telegraph.co.uk/news/obituaries/1950450/
    Irena-Sendler.html

13. http://www.bulletininserts.org/legacy.html p2-3

14. Proverbs 22:6

15. Psalm 1:6a

16. *Beckett*: John Beckett, *Mastering Monday*, (Downers Grove,
    Intervarsity Press, 2006), 67.

17. Psalm100:5

CHAPTER 6

1. John 21:22b

2. *Federer*: William J. Federer, *America's God and Country*,
   (Coppell: Fame Publishing, 1994), 655.

3. Ibid., 248.

4. Ibid., 48-49.

5. http://www.americasearch.net/index.php?date=2004-

02-03&view=View

Article defining Feb 3, 1943 in *The American Minute* "Four Chaplains Day"

6. http://www.allabouthistory.org/school-prayer.htm
7. Ibid., 2.
8. www.nccev.org?violence/statistics/statistics-school.html
9. John 8:31-32
10. Psalm 106:3
11. http://www.frc.org/get.cfm?i=WU09E09
12. Jeremiah 1:5
13. Ephesians 6:2
14. Isaiah1:17
15. Deuteronomy 15:11
16. www.rzim.org/GlobalElements/GFV/449/ ArticleID1020 "Defending Christianity in A Secular Culture" p 2
17. Ibid., paragraph 6
18. Ibid., paragraph 7
19. Psalm 33:12 NKJV
20. http://www.filmsite.org/toki.html p 2
21. http://www.imdb.com/title/tt0056592/quotes p 1
22. Ibid.
23. Ibid., 2.
24. Psalm 1:6
25. Psalm 106:7b,13,14,16, 29
26. Psalm 106:30
27. Psalm 97:2b

CHAPTER 7

1. Psalm 31:19a

2. Isaiah 40:31a

3. *Nowen*: Henri Nowen, *The Dance of Life*, (Notre Dame: Ave Marie press, 2005), 30.

4. Colossians 1:27

5. John 1:12a

6. *Foster*: Richard Foster, *Life With God* (San Francisco: Harper One, 2008), 126-127.

7. *Vogel*: Dwight W. and Linda J Vogel, *Sacramental Living* (Nashville: Upper Room Books, 1999), 21.

8. Ibid.

9. http://fum.org/QL/issues0703/radicalfaithfulness.htm

10. Isaiah 42:21

11. Psalm 31:19-20

CHAPTER 8

1. Psalm 24:3-4

2. http://bibletools.org/index.cfm/fuseaction/Bible.show/sVerseID/14245/eVerseID/14246
   John W. Rittenbaugh, The Beatitudes, Part 6: The Pure in Heart

3. *Reed*: Gerard Reed, *C.S. Lewis and the Bright Shadow of Holiness*, (Kansas City: Beacon Hill Press, 1999), 92-93.

4. I Peter 1:15

5. I Corinthians 1:9

6. *Postema*: Don Postema, *Space For God*, (Grand Rapids: CRC Publications, 1997), 181.

7. *Foster:* Richard Foster, *Celebration of Discipline*, (San Francisco: Harper Collins, 1998), 35.

8. *Cash*: Billie Cash, *PRAYERSURGE*, (Greenville, Belfast: Ambassador, 2005), 87.

9. I Corinthians 2:16

10. Psalm 31:19-20

CHAPTER 9

1. Psalm 40:12

2. Psalm 46:1

3. John 13:34

4. Romans 12:16

5. Romans 15:7

6. Galatians 6:2

7. *Cash*: Billie Cash, *Autumn Rain* (Greenville, Belfast: Ambassador, 2004), 98.

8. www.brooklyntabernacle.org/transformations/

9. Ibid.

10. Psalm 31:19-20

CHAPTER 10

1. I John 1:5

2. http://www.mysciencesite.com/optics.html Light and Optics

3. Psalm 112:4

4. Psalm 19:8

5. Psalm 43:3

6. http://newscenter.lbl.gov/press-releases/2008/11/25/

mother-of-pearl- Mother of Pearl Secret Revealed-- Berkeley News Center

7. http://clifton.mech.northwestern.educ/-espinosa/ Papers/SEM-Nacre.pdf
   Elastic Properties of Nacre Aragonite Tablets

8. *Cash*: Billie Cash, *Light Breaking Through*, (Belfast, Greenville: Ambassador, 2003), 15.

9. Proverbs 4:18

10. http://www.australian-news.com.au/greatest_dad.htm

11. Ibid.

12. Ibid.

13. Psalm 38:10

14. Psalm 18:28

15. Psalm 36:9b

16. Psalm 118:27a

17. Proverbs 13:9a

18. Psalm 31:19-20

19. Proverbs 13:9

CHAPTER II

1. *Lane*: Dermot A. Lane, *Experience of God*; An Invitation to Do Theology, (Mahwah: Paulist Press, 2005), 78-79.

2. Ibid.

3. John 1:12 RSV

4. http://www.katapi.org.uk/ChristianFaith/IV.htm
   The Christian faith: Chapter 4 "The Transcendence and Immanence of God."

5. Ibid.

6. Proverbs 16:3

7. II Thessalonians 5:24

8. Isaiah 30:15b

9. *Cash*: Billie Cash, *A Pillow on the Highway*, (Belfast, Greenville: Ambassador, 2007), 107, 109.

10. *Tolstoy*: Leo Tolstoy, *A Confession* translated by Aylmer Maude, (Mineola; Dover, 2005), 3.

11. Ibid., 53.

12. Deuteronomy 4:29

13. Acts 17:28

14. Psalm 31:19-20

CHAPTER 12

1. Psalm 90:2

2. Isaiah 40:28-29

3. *Prince*: Derek Prince, *Entering The Presence of God*, (New Kensington: Whittaker House, 2007), 79.

4. Ecclesiastes 3:11

5. http://www.wholesomewords.org
Mary Slessor, Scottish missionary Nigeria Africa- Missionary biography copied by Stephen Ross for Wholesome Words. org. *Livingstone*: W. P. Livingstone, *Mary Slessor of Calabar, Pioneer Missionary*, (New York: George H. Doran Co. 1917), 4.

6. Ibid., 5.

7. http://www.wholesomewords.org
Copied and edited by Stephen Ross for Wholesome

Words.org Harrison: Eugene Myers Harrison, (Chicago: Scripture Press Book Division, 1949) Section II

8. Ibid.

9. *Hillman:* Os Hillman, *The Upside of Adversity,* (Ventura; Regal, 2006), 179.

10. Isaiah 26:4 NKJV

11. Psalm 31:19-20

CHAPTER 13

1. John 17:6-11,17, 20

2. Ephesians 4:15-16 NLV

3. Romans 12:5 NLT

4. http://en.wikipedia.org/wikiWatchman_Nee

5. Matthew 18:20 NLT

6. Ephesians 4:15-16

7. Psalm 42:1

8. *Buchanan:* Mark Buchanan, *Things Unseen* (Sisters: Multnomah, 2002), 50.

9. http://bible.ca/ef/expository-ezekiel-37-1-3.htm

10. Ezekiel 37: 1-3

11. Ezekiel 37:4 NLT

12. Ezekiel 37:5b NLT

13. Ezekiel 37:9 NLT

14. Ezekiel 37:27 NLT

15. *Foster:* Richard Foster, *Life With God,* (San Francisco: Harper One, 2008), 182.

16. *Fullerton:* W. Y. Fullerton, D.D., *F. B. Meyer, A Biography,*

(Streetsville: Ontario Christian Books, 1992), 7.

17. Ibid., 212.

18. *Lewis:* C. S. Lewis, *The Chronicles of Narnia: The Lion, The Witch and The Wardrobe* illustrated by Pauline Baynes, (New York; Harper Trophy, 2001), 79-80.

19. Ibid., 126.

20. Matthew 6:33

21. Psalm 93:1

22. Psalm 31:19-20

CHAPTER 14

1. Genesis 17:1 HCS

2. Genesis 17:1 NKJV

3. http://therealpresence.org/eucharst/into/livingpg.htm John Harden, S.J.

4. Psalm 31:8b

5. *Merton:* Thomas Merton, *The Climate of Monastic Prayer,* p149 as quoted in *Space For God,* Don Postema 1997.

6. *Nelson:* Portia Nelson, *Me In You and You In Me,* (London: Souvenir Press, 2004), 99.

7. Psalm 16:8-9 NKJV

8. Psalm 31: 19-20

9. Isaiah 62:6a

10. Proverbs 15:3NKJV

11. Psalm 73:26b,28

12. *Sherwood:* Ben Sherwood, *The Survivors Club,* (New York: Grand Central Publishing, 2009), 317.

13. Judges 6:7b–10

14. Judges 6:12

15. Judges 6:14

16. Judges 6:15

17. Judges 6:16

18. Judges 7:2c

19. II Corinthians 12:9

20. *Foster:* Richard Foster, *Life With God*, (New York; Harper Collins, 2008), 200.

21. *Bingham*: Derick Bingham, *The Brontes, Veins Running Fire,* (Belfast: Ambassador, 2007), 216.

22. http://www.exsmo.com/museum/people/tripp/tripp.htm

23. *McManus*: Erwin Raphael McManus, *Uprising*, (Nashville: Thomas Nelson, 2003), 126.

OTHER BOOKS BY BILLIE CASH

Windows Of Assurance

In her Journey of Prayer, Billie Cash shares the resources she used to persevere as a school girl in 33 different schools. Those experiences propelled Billie into the artificial light of the theater; but it was the penetrating light of God's presence that birthed identity and ready resolve. For each window she opened, His love met her with grace and called her to test the real release of prevailing prayer.

ISBN: 1-889893-59-5

$12.99/£8.99 (224 pp)

Light Breaking Through

Light. The visible reminder of Invisible Light. (T. S. Eliot) The light of God searches all things, our struggles, loneliness and brokenness. This book lets us experience that light, as it breaks through our struggles, intercepting us with truth, love, and fresh insights at every turn, in every season. He urges us onward, to continue, to grow, to believe, to love, and to finish our race, giving us illumination in the darkest days. We can trust His Light.

ISBN: 1-889893-97-8

$9.99/£6.99 (144 pp)

Autumn Rain

This book is a message of faith's journey, having a beginning, becoming dependent, being responsible, fruitful and then transforming the landscape through transplanted lives. The metaphor of the garden is carried throughout the book; beginning faith is nurtured by Spring rain but transforming faith has a harvest, an abundance brought by the autumn rain, the rain of harvest. It is a faith that continues to change the landscape of life.

ISBN: 1-932307-33-8

$11.99/£7.99 (224 pp)

Prayersurge

Billie writes as she lives — in bursts of glorious energy. With her concise, almost poetic style, she pulls us into this beautiful description of the work of prayer in a Christian's life. Her heart for God is revealed. Be careful as you read — this is a short book but the message is large — hear the call! Rise up in prayer! Love God! Love others! Be transformed!

ISBN: 1-932307-41-9

$10.99/£8.99 (160 pp)

A Pillow on the Highway

Children are at peace when those who care for them have learned to rest in God's loving arms. I know this because long before my mother wrote this book I saw her live its truth. A Pillow on the Highway is a living, breathing exposition of Jeremiah 6:16, which brings into the brightest focus what the author has lived for decades and what God Almighty intends us to experience every day...a treasure of truth and testimony that will transform your life.

— LCDR Carey Cash, US Navy Chaplain, author of A Table in the Presence; Naples, Italy

ISBN: 978-1-932307-80-1

$10.99/£8.99 (144 pp)